About the Author

Tim Gavin is an Episcopal priest who serves as the School Chaplain at The Episcopal Academy located in Newtown Square, Pennsylvania. His ministry includes teaching, providing pastoral care, leading worship, and overseeing the school's Haiti Partnership Program. He is the liaison of the US Haiti Partnership Program for the National Association of Episcopal Schools. His essays and poems have appeared in Anglican Theological Review, Grow Christians, Poetry South, The Cresset, Plough Quarterly, and other journals. His book of poems, Lyrics from the Central Plateau, was published by Prolific Press. He lives with his wife, Joyce, in southeastern Pennsylvania.

A Radical Beginning: A Journey through the Prayer of St. Francis

Tim Gavin

A Radical Beginning: A Journey through the Prayer of St. Francis

Olympia Publishers
London

www.olympiapublishers.com
OLYMPIA PAPERBACK EDITION

Copyright © Tim Gavin 2023

The right of Tim Gavin to be identified as author of
this work has been asserted in accordance with sections 77 and 78 of
the Copyright, Designs and Patents Act 1988.

All Rights Reserved

No reproduction, copy or transmission of this publication
may be made without written permission.
No paragraph of this publication may be reproduced,
copied or transmitted save with the written permission of the publisher,
or in accordance with the provisions
of the Copyright Act 1956 (as amended).

Any person who commits any unauthorized act in relation to
this publication may be liable to criminal
prosecution and civil claims for damage.

A CIP catalogue record for this title is
available from the British Library.

ISBN: 978-1-80439-385-7

This is a spiritual memoir. Names, characters, places and incidents
have been changed to protect the identity of any person identified in
this book.

First Published in 2023

Olympia Publishers
Tallis House
2 Tallis Street
London
EC4Y 0AB

Printed in Great Britain

Dedication

Gratitude and love to my wife, Joyce, who keeps me grounded and inspires me to discern my own radical beginning. Also for my two sons, Jake and Nick, who are on their own journey to discover their own radical beginning.

Acknowledgements

Acknowledgment is due to the following editors and congregations where some form of the scenarios within this book were first unveiled: Grow Christians, Plough Quarterly, St. Alban's Church (Newtown Square, PA), The Episcopal Academy, Church of the Redeemer (Longport, NJ), and St. Marc's School in Cerca, Haiti. Aslo, I would like to offer a note of gratitude to Courtney Brinkerhoff-Rau who offered her talents and expertise to proofread the text.

Prologue

Preach the Gospel. Sometimes use word. This maxim attributed to St. Francis of Assisi reminds us that our words mean little if our actions contradict them. Jesus knew this. The Great Cloud of Witnesses knew this. We know it, but don't always live into it. In addition, St. Francis instinctually embodies the verse from Deuteronomy, "One does not live by bread alone, but by every word that comes from the mouth of the Lord." Perhaps there lies the reason he so readily gave away all his possessions, picked up his cross, and followed Christ.

St. Francis who lived the Gospel literally provides us with the most beautiful prayer that sums up the entire teachings of Jesus. St. Francis condenses all the teachings of Jesus into thirteen sentences, giving us a blueprint for Gospel living. St. Francis knew intrinsically what Jesus tried to teach his disciples after the feeding of the 5000, "The Spirit gives life; the flesh is useless." St. Francis embodied the spirit of Christ in all that he did. He saw beyond the trappings of the flesh and allowed the image of God within himself to reach out to embrace the image of God in others. That sums up the reality of living in the spirit, engaging the image of God in others. Obviously easier said than done.

The Prayer of St. Francis provides a gentle reminder: "If we," in the words of William Law, "are to follow Christ, then we must make it our common way of spending every day". The prayer guides our intentions so all that we do may glorify God while we live out our earthly life. The prayer requires no prerequisite skills, degrees, or experience. However, following the prayer will lead us to a righteous life and a life full of wisdom. The acquired wisdom can be shared and spread to build God's kingdom here on Earth.

I have known this prayer since childhood. However, on a certain Christmas Eve during my late 50's, the prayer brought me a certain joy that one can only experience as if one received a fresh start, a spiritual reset, or as I like to say, *a radical beginning.* In the pages of this short book, I am inviting the reader to join me in exploring the depth and wisdom of the Prayer Attributed to St. Francis.

The Prayer Attributed to St. Francis

Lord make us instruments of your peace. Where there is hatred, let us sow love; where there is injury; pardon; where there is discord, union; where there is doubt, faith; where there is despair, hope; where there is sadness, joy. Grant that we may not so much seek to be consoled as to console; to be understood as to understand; to be loved as to love. For it is in giving that we receive; it is in pardoning that we are pardoned; and it is in dying that we are born to eternal life. Amen.

Chapter 1

A Preface to Peace

Radical Beginning

One Christmas Eve, during the great pandemic, I was supporting the rector, Fr. Matt, at St. Alban's Church with our drop-in/drive by Christmas Eve Service. Fr. Matt gave out communion and I offered blessings. An elderly man came up to me and asked me to recite The Prayer of St. Francis for his Christmas blessing. I responded, "I know the prayer, but I don't think I could recite it for you. I am embarrassed to say, 'I don't have it memorized. I'm sorry.' He waved his hand at me saying, "Just give me a regular blessing."

After he left, I had time to wait until the next family arrived, so I went to the Book of Common Prayer and found the Prayer of St. Francis. I began to read it. However, I never read it with such urgency and desire to know the prayer. I analyzed every line of it, every phrase of it, every word of it. I wanted to consume the prayer and make it part of me. The spirit of the prayer initiated for me a journey toward a radical beginning – the same radical beginning that Jesus offers Nicodemus on another dark night.

On that Christmas Eve, I felt that God offered me an opportunity to start anew, to establish a new beginning, one that was radical. For me, the radical beginning of which I speak allows us to find the roots of our origin and the origin that is based on God's creation and God's creation of humankind in the

Divine Image. As I dove into the prayer, I thought, "my goodness, the beauty and simplicity of this prayer has escaped me for so many years". At that moment, I realized I found the opportunity to meet myself in God.

Now, I reflect on the exchange between Jesus and Nicodemus and how Nicodemus failed to understand the meaning of Jesus' offer to be *born from above*. I sense that John, the evangelist, was echoing the first creation story when he developed this scene. In the beginning, when God created the universe and created humankind in God's image, humans enjoyed all the divine possibilities available to them. In the beginning, humankind shared an intimate relationship with God. A relationship built on peace and the future possibilities that God and humankind would coexist in perpetuity. However, through Adam and Eve, humankind decided to break the bond and forfeit our intimate relationship with God. Therefore, we entered into the world of sin, which obfuscates the Divine Image within us.

Nevertheless, God refused and refuses to give up on humankind. Through Jesus Christ, God offers for us to engage in *a radical beginning* where the faith of Christ ensures *the world might be saved through him.* On that night, I realized this short prayer offers us a passage to a radical beginning that delivers us from the darkness of sin and procures for us the light of Christ.

In actuality, the prayer woke me up to the reality of what Christianity is all about. How it calls us to live a godly life, a life that is in this world and draws us toward a righteous relationship with God and other human beings. It reminds us of the essence of the Gospel message to repent and believe in the good news because forgiveness is at hand. It calls us into solidarity with other people – rich and poor, young and old, strong and weak. It calls us into restoration with God and with one another. It mimics the personal qualities exhibited by Jesus throughout the gospels. Since that night, I have memorized the prayer, so I can recite it anytime, anywhere.

As I studied the prayer for days on end, I discovered this short prayer contains four movements. Each movement finds its impetus in scripture. I realized The Prayer Attributed to St. Francis finds its source in the biblical teachings from both the Old and New Testament. Just as scripture contains all things necessary for salvation, so too does this prayer. I came to realize that if I could live up to the aspirations of this prayer, then I would be living as Christ desires me to live.

Scriptural Reflection: A Radical Beginning

Genesis provides profound insight into the roots of our beginning. If we look to the first creation story, we find that we, both male and female, are created in God's image. The critical question becomes, *"What does this mean?"* Some say we inherited God's Divine Nature, and therefore resemble God. Others answer this to mean we possess some of the same qualities of God such as the power to love, to destroy, and to procreate images of ourselves. However, I prefer to believe the Divine Image we share leads us to stand right with God. I believe that our faith in Christ provides us an opportunity to enter into our radical beginning when righteousness guarantees eternal life and an intimate relationship with God. That's when we enter into the *peace the surpasses all understanding* and live devout lives, which lead us to responding to our faith by "performing acts of charity promptly, diligently, and frequently."[1]

Our radical beginning that we achieve through Faith in Christ allows us to become who God wants us authentically to

---

[1] Introduction to the Devout Life by Francis de Sales

be. Being made in God's image and living into the inheritance allows us to focus on godly attributes such as love, grace, joy, charity, and peace. If we look at Christ in the Gospels, we find Jesus is one with The Father. Jesus says, "The Father and I are one" (John 10:30). When we live into our Divine Image, we, too, become one with The Father and with Jesus. Ultimately, the radical beginning Christ offers us through peace takes us on a journey where we can fully live into our Divine Image in which our Divine Nature respects the Divine Nature in others. In the end, our radical beginning and accepting it allows us to begin anew in which we truly follow our baptismal vow to "respect the dignity of every human being".

Questions for Further Discussion

1. How do we live into our Divine Image on a daily basis?

2. Other than Genesis 1 and John 3, how can scripture provide us an understanding of our radical beginning?

3. In terms of our tradition, what examples from our history can guide us to live into the peace that surpasses all understanding?

4. What does peace look like for us as individuals and as a Christian community?

Chapter 2

Advocacy and the Pursuit of Peace

The First Movement: A Call to Instigate Peace
    The first movement is the opening line in which we ask God to make us "instruments of peace." The rest of the prayer gives us a rubric to follow. Let's face it, we cannot pursue peace by waging war. Violence in our language and our actions only leads to more violence. Insulting someone, talking behind a person's back, or striking someone will never lead to peace. It may lead to submission and a false claim of peace, but these acts of violence will never lead to authentic peace. I recall strict disciplinarians I had in grammar and high school. They tried to catch us making poor decisions and hammered us. They focused on retributive justice, making sure we paid a heavy price for falling short. They applied fear and "violence" as a strategy to keep us in line. We stayed in line not because we had changed as students, but because we feared retaliation. I remember one teacher in particular who used intimidation, threats, and physical assaults to force us to toe the line. According to her own assessment, she ran a tight ship, and no one was permitted to rock *her* boat. In essence, she prided herself on "whipping us into shape." She immersed herself as an autocratic authority figure who would take no prisoners and ruled with an iron fist. Of course, we behaved when we were in her view, but we did not do the right thing from a sense of righteousness but more out of sordid

submission. The peace that this teacher manufactured in her classroom obtained its source from violence, and violence never leads to authentic peace. The atmosphere of the classroom embodied anxiety and failed to nurture true learning where risks were freely taken. The teacher, in her need to control and manufacture discipline (i.e. peace), fostered stagnation rather than creativity, recitation rather than critical thinking, and teacher-centered monologues rather than student-centered expression. Sadly, the teacher failed to create a sense of community. Each student felt isolated on an island, abandoned, and somehow orphaned.

Interestingly, Jesus promises in John's Gospel that he will not leave his disciples orphaned. He promises, "The Advocate, the Holy Spirit, whom the Father will send in my name, will teach you everything, and remind you of all that I have said to you. Peace I leave with you; my peace I give to you. I do not give to you as the world gives. Do not let your hearts be troubled, and do not let them be afraid." Through faith in Christ, we are never alone. We can rely on *the* Advocate. Therefore, we carry with us the peace of Christ and with that reality comes the Holy Spirit who teaches us the wisdom we need to have in order to obtain true peace. True peace relies on our willingness *to turn the other cheek, to love our enemies,* and to be willing to *lay down one's life for one's friend.* In reality, peace comes with a price but a much greater reward than violence.

Peace provides the opportunity for humanity to live into its inherited Diving Image where we share intimacy with God and with one another. We witness this when Jesus meets the Samaritan woman at the well. The exchange reveals that Jesus knows this woman. He knows all the intimate details of her life. As a result, he helps her to come to see herself as she truly is and, in the process, she comes to know Jesus as the Christ.

We need to realize that the exchange between Jesus and the Samaritan woman exists in front of a backdrop of social constructs of gender, creed, and ethnicity. Since Jesus approaches her without a hint of judgment and with more of an all-out effort of acceptance and inclusion, the scene avoids the violence that could have precipitated from a typical encounter between a Jewish man and a Samaritan woman in mid daylight. Due to Jesus acting as an agent of God's peace, the woman becomes empowered to accept herself just as Jesus does and becomes empowered to proclaim the messiahship of Jesus. She becomes – very much like John the Baptist in chapter 1 – a witness to the true messiah, the Lamb of God.

Peace unfolds because Jesus broke down the barriers that existed among men and women, Jews and Samaritans, and the unrighteous and righteous. Jesus offers her the same thing he offered Nicodemus. She accepts. Her faith in Jesus as the Christ ensures her the power and strength to leave behind her "bucket," which may symbolize her willingness to let go of her past life, her mistakes, her sins and rely on "the water that [Jesus] will give" and "will become in [her] a spring of water gushing up to eternal life." She runs to her village as a new woman, reborn into a radical beginning, who is liberated by her conversion and, as a result, experiences a spiritual transformation. Consequently, she willingly draws others into her newfound faith in Christ. That's where true peace leads when adhering to the will of God.

We can imagine that the first movement, *Lord, make me an instrument of your peace,* may contain the implied question of "How?" The next movement begins to answer the question, "How can I act as an instrument of peace?" The answer proves revolutionary.

However, before moving on, let's examine the life of St. Francis and how he became an instrument of peace, which opened for him the path to show respect for all people and all of creation. Francis transcended the limits of the church, the church being a product of its times. He went to the Middle East to reach out to the Muslim world and according to Karen Armstrong[2], he "showed the Muslim world respect, which went beyond the self-righteous hatred and rivalry that frequently afflicts institutional religion while maintaining loyalty to the Church." In all that St. Francis did, he preserved peace.

When St. Francis "falls in love with Lady Poverty" and begged for his food, he would respond to his father's curses and insults with blessings. When people ridiculed him for rebuilding San Damiano, he prayed. When he was beaten and robbed, he embraced Christ's passion. In all that he did, St. Francis pursued peace.

Scriptural Application: "What is your name" (Mark 5)?

"What is your name?" This simple question leads Jesus into a full relationship with the Gerasene Demoniac. The man suffered from possession and people tried to control him by isolating him to the tombs and putting him in chains. These responses failed to help the man, nor did they help the townspeople. Jesus steps out of the boat and before he can feel firm footing, the man "ran out of the tombs to meet him." We could read this as the man wanting help, even if his demons didn't. The man bows before Jesus and screams, "What have you to do with me, Jesus, Son of the Most High God? I adjure you by

---

[2] Francis of Assisi: A revolutionary Life by Karen Armstrong and Adrian House

God, do not torment me." I find this an interesting request because it seems predicated upon the fact that the man expects Jesus to torment him. Perhaps this is due to the reality that the man lived every day among the tombs. The townspeople, due to their fear of him, tormented him by putting him in chains and keeping him isolated. As a result, the man, even in his darkest pain, expects more from Jesus. The soothing question of Jesus asking his name introduces a peaceful moment which leads to a dialogue that is manifested in the man's restoration to sanity. Jesus even responds to the Legion of Demons with peace by granting their request to "send them into the swine." The peace brought to the man as a free gift from the grace of Christ has the man sitting quietly, fully clothed, and in his right mind; but, sadly, when the townspeople see him sitting quietly, they fail to understand the peace. In an ironic twist, the townspeople who tried to control the man and witnessed what Jesus had done ask Jesus to leave their neighborhood.

What do the townspeople fear? They try to address the madness of the man by attempting to control and subdue him. They clearly see him as something or someone worthy of marginalization. Instead of treating the cause of the man's torment, they isolate him and dehumanize him, saying that he is not worthy of being alive. Therefore, they imprison him among the tombs. They rely on violence instead of instigating peace. They succumb to the instruments of oppression and psychological warfare and project their own fears onto the man and ultimately onto Jesus as well.

Jesus, on the contrary, chooses to address the man with a peaceful heart. Jesus, even despite the man's madness, respects his individual dignity. As a result, he ministers to the needs of the man in a loving, tender way. He initiates personal contact with

"What is your name?" This small gesture insinuates that Jesus wants to know who the man is and sees the man beyond the chains and lack of clothing. Jesus calms the man, not with strategies of violence, but with constructs of peace.

Questions for Further Discussion

1. When have you observed that efforts to find peaceful resolutions to "madness" are met with fear and resistance?

2. We are well versed in the instruments of war, what are the instruments of peace?

3. What areas of our personal life (i.e., demons, relationships, poor habits) need a peaceful intervention?

4. How can we move beyond personal and communal rivalry to attain peaceful co-existence?

Chapter 3

The One Who Sows

The Second Movement

As Anglicans, we inherit a great wealth of wisdom from scripture, tradition, and reason. This authority provides us with insight into how to live a goldy or Christ-centered life. The Great Commandment: "Love God with all your heart, soul, and strength and to love your neighbor as yourself," embodies all we need to know. In this, we possess the keystone to righteous living. In addition, the ministry of Jesus provides us with an example to follow. Jesus says, "I am among you as one who serves." In addition to scripture, the great cloud of witnesses provides us a tradition of saintly self-denial, which enable many women and men to pick up their crosses to follow Christ. St. Francis and St. Clare provide excellent witness to follow the Gospel, literally through self-denial and by glorifying God in all their actions. Finally, great minds provide sound reason. We have from Paul to Origen; from Augustine to Aquinas; from William Law to the Wesley brothers; and from Frances Perkins to Barbara Taylor Brown who provide for us good reasons to live a life that brings us in alignment to God's will. The second movement of The Prayer Attributed to St. Francis provides a simple pattern of actions that lead to peace.

Sowing Love

The Second movement of the prayer provides a list of positive or revolutionary actions to help us respond to the brokenness of our world. To sow love where there is hatred is a difficult command. However, sowing love will yield more love. Love is the only way to undo and erase hatred. If we are to live into our true nature of being made in God's image, then we need to imitate our creator, "for the LORD is good; his steadfast love endures forever, and his faithfulness to all generations."

As Psalm 100 reveals, God remains steadfast in his love for all people through thick and thin. Consequently, God's love remains faithful "to all generations." God's love flows freely; therefore, we, too, must allow our love to flow freely from our central being to others.

However, love requires action. It demands that we sow specific behaviors as well as attitudes. Our attitudes about people may create within us negative assumptions of people who differ from us. We may rely on different media resources to fill in the blanks for us, which in a way falsely frees us from engaging with others who are different and discovering that we may in fact have more in common than previously understood.

I wonder if the love for others championed by the scriptures becomes romanticized in our minds and, consequently, develops into an empty platitude. How often do we hear *love your neighbor* and fail to comprehend all it encompasses? How often do we fail to expand the definition of our neighbor to make it entirely inclusive of all people, even our enemies? So, we have *neighbor* as one side of it, then we turn to *love*. Do we truly take to heart how we must love our neighbor? Are we ready for the inconvenience love demands? Are we prepared to lay down our life as a symbol of our love? How often do we even ask ourselves these questions?

We can look to Jesus to help shape our answers to these questions. Jesus approaches people with an inner eye to acknowledge that they are made in God's image. One night, a Pharisee invites Jesus to dinner. A woman with a questionable profession arrives at the house and begins to anoint Jesus' feet. She kissed his feet and washed them with her tears, drying them with her hair. This interaction between the woman and Jesus created a disturbing scene and the Pharisee thought to himself, "If this man were a prophet, he would have known who and what kind of woman this is who is touching him – that she is a sinner." The Pharisee sits in judgment of both the woman and Jesus. He reveals his self-righteous attitude and assesses the scene from a position of Law as opposed to the position of love. He appears to be self-pleased because he concludes that there can't be anything special about Jesus. However, Jesus refuses to become defensive. Instead, he tells a story of a creditor who forgives the debts of two people. One person owed him five hundred denarii and the other fifty. Jesus asks the Pharisee, "Now which of the debtors will love the creditor more?"

The Pharisee responds, "I suppose the one for whom he canceled the greater debt." After the Pharisee responds correctly, Jesus explains to him that "this woman" treated Jesus with greater respect and love than the host of the dinner. Jesus points out to the Pharisee, "I entered your house; you gave me no water for my feet, but she has bathed my feet with her tears and dried them wither hair. You gave me no kiss, but from the time I came in she has not stopped kissing my feet. You did not anoint my head with oil, but she has anointed my feet with ointment. Therefore, I tell you, her sins, which were many, have been forgiven; hence she has shown great love." Jesus offers a cryptic message, "But the one to whom little is forgiven, loves little." Jesus then turns to the woman and forgives all of her sins. The guest at the dinner who are religious leaders become appalled and say to themselves, "Who is this who even forgives sins?" They are flabbergasted. Jesus then says to the woman, "Your faith has saved you; go in peace."

The woman acts from a place of faith. She does not enter the house expecting anything in return. She offers her love to Jesus and in response she is redeemed. The Pharisee and the other guests in the house fail to act on faith but solely sit on the seat of judgment. They use the Law to elevate themselves, believing that they are worthy of Jesus' presence just because of who they are and the position they hold in society. They stand right with themselves, whereas the woman stands right with God. Love leads to redemption and with redemption we, like the woman, can *go in peace.*

Scriptural Application: Joseph's Growth (Genesis 37 – 50)

For all of Joseph's foibles as a young man, he became transformed after being sold into slavery. His brothers despised him because Jacob favored him among all of his sons. Joseph reveled in this and bragged that they one day would be bowing down to him. We could say Joseph hit rock bottom literally and figuratively. His brothers put him in a dry well and then sold him to the Ishmaelites. The Ishmaelites sold him to Potiphar, a captain of the Pharaoh's guard. The work Joseph performed for Potiphar brought many blessings to the house of Potiphar. As a result, Potiphar "left all that he had in Joseph's charge; and, with him there, he had no concern for anything but the food that he ate." As time went on, Joseph caught Potiphar's wife's eye. She made advances toward Joseph because "he was handsome and good looking." She pressed him and said,

"'Lie with me.' But he refused and said to his master's wife, 'Look, with me here, my master has no concern about anything in the house, and he has put everything that he has in my hand. He is not greater in this house than I am, nor has he kept back anything from me except yourself, because you are his wife. How then could I do this great wickedness, and sin against God?'"

From the time Joseph spied on his brothers in Genesis 37 to the time he was sold to Potiphar, he transformed from selfishness to selflessness because he knew the love of God. Joseph becomes the first person in The Bible to advance the notion of *relational theology*. He comprehends that a sin against Potiphar and his wife was also a sin against God. He comes to provide us with the reality that our love for God is manifested in our love for others.

Joseph refuses her advances and suffers the consequences. She accuses him of rape. As a result, he is thrown into prison. He does not protest the accusation. The question as to why lingers in my mind. Perhaps, Joseph knows that his words won't be accepted as truthful testimony. Perhaps, Joseph realizes if he were to speak up, Potiphar's wife would be put to death. As a result, he shows mercy by accepting the punishment and goes to jail. He intuitively understands, "If I do this great wickedness, then I will sin against God."

Each time I read or teach the Joseph Narrative, I examine it as a story of transformation. I love witnessing Joseph's change from a self-centered seventeen-year-old boy to a thoughtful other-centered adult, who is able to give of himself, offer mercy, and come to terms with his past in a graceful manner. In the end, Joseph uses his intelligence to save Egypt from devastation and uses the love in his heart to honor God and forgive his brothers.

Questions for Further Discussion

1. How do we, in our daily life, demonstrate our love for God through our interactions with our neighbors?

2. Can you think of someone who is different from you in terms of race, politics, gender, religion or any other identifier and write a list of your similarities?

3. Where in our lives does faith transcend the laws by which we live?

4. How do we live into the Anglican ethos of relational theology? What are the barriers that prevent us from loving our neighbors? What are our blind spots? Where do we need to grow?

Sowing Pardon

We all have been injured one way or another. However, the loving and peaceful way to respond to injury is not through retaliation but through pardoning. After all, forgiveness leads to forgiveness. Mercy begets mercy. Consequently, I think about all the times I sought forgiveness and was greeted by grace. Also, I am reminded by the baptismal Covenant I always need to be willing to forgive.

The eight and ninth Steps of the twelve Step Program may prove to be the most challenging steps toward recovery. One must admit the wrongs done to another person due to alcohol consumption. This inventory demands self-reflection and an honest admission of one's flaws. Once the individual completes a comprehensive list, she goes on to Step nine and makes amends with the person. However, this also requires discernment because one can only seek forgiveness if it will not cause greater pain to the victim. During Step nine one makes oneself vulnerable by surrendering control over the situation and by giving the control of the process to the victim who then can decide to forgive or not to forgive.

When we injure someone, we need to own the harm. However, God demands that we become advocates of those who experience injury. We must stand up and speak out against oppression while still loving the oppressor. This becomes a delicate balancing act. Jesus provides a way to sow pardon where there is injury. When the Scribes and Pharisees put before Jesus a woman caught in adultery, Jesus responds to the injury that she committed and the injury to the crowd, who at this point already held stones in their hand, by offering pardon. Jesus demonstrates great wisdom in navigating the fine line between Law and Mercy. By all accounts, she seems painted into a corner when the Scribes and Pharisees recite, "The Law of Moses commands us to stone the woman." I imagine Jesus responds in his own head, "Yes. That's true." He buys times by writing in the sand. We don't know what he is writing. On the surface he wants to avoid the question completely but they keep "questioning him." In a sense, he is forced to draw a conclusion and give them a valid response, one based on The Law of Moses. He stands up and responds, "Let anyone among you who is without sin be the first to throw a stone at her." He then bends down and continues to write in the sand. Ancient manuscripts add "the sins of each of them." As a result, Jesus sows pardon by demonstrating that we all need pardon. Even the best of us.

When I think of the times that I may have caused injury, I wonder how I would have reacted if the person to whom I caused injury just turned the other cheek. Would the act of turning the other cheek completely unarm me, causing me to reorient my thinking from "the only way to relate to a person is through violence," to realize that the best way to relate to a person is through gentleness? However, this notion places the responsibility on the victim. I can now ask, what injury have I caused? Have I caused an injury of the heart or body, the spirit or flesh? Have I made a person feel inferior, unwanted, or isolated? These injuries of the spirit may inflict more pain than any injury of the body.

Jesus' sermon on the mount causes us to reflect on how we carry out God's Law. Do we follow the letter of Law by proclaiming, *I never killed anyone* or *stole anything*? Does this lead us to believe that since we avoided breaking these two commandments, we are somehow righteous? As Christians, we know from the mouth of Jesus that the best way to live into the commandments requires us to love God with our entire heart, soul, and strength and to love our neighbor as ourselves. In other words, what we do to our neighbor, we likewise do to God. The first Letter of John drives this point home, when it states, "Those who say, 'I love God,' and hate their brothers or sisters, are liars; for those who do not love a brother or sister whom they have seen, cannot love God whom they have not seen." The Law of Christianity comes down to this simple reality. Perhaps, St. Francis exemplified that more than anyone when he set out to the Middle East to bring about peace during the wars between Christians and Muslims. If we had only listened to him. He tried to sow pardon where there was injury.

How do we today follow his example? Do we try to sow pardon where the wounds of racism, bigotry, and sexism have caused an imbalance of access to equal opportunity in our society? Just as Jesus broke down barriers between men and women, Jews and gentiles, the righteous and unrighteous, we possess an opportunity each day to do the same. We can ensure that people enjoy the same privileges we enjoy. I remember one time I visited a church as a parishioner. The sun rose and shined through the windows of the tiny seventeenth century church. The church held years of tears, laughter, dancing and mourning. The charm emanated from the stone walls and the wooden pews. I felt like I was in another era. I entered a pew in which a woman was already occupying.

"Good morning," I offered. "Happy Sunday."

She looked at me and rolled her eyes. I sat down next to her. Her pocketbook was the only thing separating us in the tiny pew. She looked at me, looked at her pocketbook, and looked back at me and then moved her pocketbook to her other side. I chuckled, thinking, "Do you think I am going to take your pocketbook and run?" I reflected on her action and thought, "What an odd response. What if I were an African American person? Would I think she was moving her pocketbook because she feared I was going to steal it because I was a Black man? I think if I were Black, then I would arrive at that conclusion." This made me realize that she didn't think I would steal her pocketbook due to the color of my skin but for some other reason. I had the privilege to dismiss her action as ignorance on her part. I felt no judgment nor did I have to carry around the stigma she might have associated with my skin color. The question becomes, how can I share the same privilege with others knowing that I am not judged due to the color of my skin?

On one hand, the answer is simple. On the other hand, the execution of the answer proves difficult. The answer leads me to breaking down as many barriers that exist between me and others. It means inviting others into my circle and sharing my privileges with others. It means becoming vulnerable by entering the circle of others to see the world through their eyes. In other words, learning empathy. The execution of doing so may come at a cost. Your friends, co-workers, or family members may not see a need to empathize with the marginalized. As a result, you may suffer ridicule, ostracization, and worse. For example, once I became more active in support issues surrounding diversity, equity, and inclusion, some people stopped associating with me or labeled me a socialist, rebel-rouser, and radical. As a result, when we attempt to sow pardon amidst injury, we need to prepare to sow the same pardon with the people who react negatively to our following the gospel. The result of such work may cause discord; therefore, we need to always keep our vision on the union that Christ enjoys with the Father and Holy Spirit.

Scriptural Application: "Neither Do I Condemn You" (John 8)

Early one morning, Jesus came to the Temple. He wasn't there for long when a group of Pharisees and Scribes brought before him a woman who had committed adultery. They threw her at his feet and said, "Teacher, this woman was caught in the very act of committing adultery. Now, in the law, Moses commanded us to stone such women. Now, what do you say?"

It is obvious that they were attempting to entrap him, so that they could accuse him of blasphemy and violating The Law. He bends down and draws in the sand as if he is distancing himself from them and giving himself time to think. The delay in his response builds some suspense. Do the Pharisees and Scribes finally have him? While he continues to draw in the sand, they keep questioning him. Finally, he stands and delivers the famous, "Let anyone among you who is without sin be the first to throw a stone at her." He stoops down again and continues to write in the sand. Some scholars suggest that he is enumerating their individual sins. One by one they drop their stones and leave. "Jesus was left alone with the woman standing before him. Jesus straightened up and said to her, "Woman, where are they? Has no one condemned you?" She said, "No one, sir." And Jesus said, "Neither do I condemn you. Go your way, and from now on do not sin again."

Jesus offers compassion and pardon in a situation where the Law demanded an eye for an eye response. She committed adultery. She deserved death. However, Jesus looked beyond the actions which made her fall short of righteousness and saw a person who was in great need of mercy not punishment. He also saw an angry mob in its self-righteous indignation desiring to use The Law not for righteousness but for their own purposes in order to gain power, authority, and control over Jesus. They were hoping to injure Jesus' ministry, following, and reputation; however, Jesus' application of pardon foiled their attempt. In a matter of fact, Jesus demonstrated tenderness to both the woman and the accusers. He didn't take the "holier than thou approach" with either party. His tenderness reflects a pastoral approach to the situation in which his theological view of lovIng God with his entire heart, soul, and mind led to loving his neighbors – all of them. He was in a position where he could have had the woman stoned. He also held the high moral ground, knowing the sins of the accusers, and could have chastised and castigated them for being self-righteous. Instead, he led them to where they needed to go: a place where they acknowledged their own blind spots. In the end, Jesus saw injury and sowed pardon. In the end, as Christians, we are forgiven as we forgive others.

Questions for Further Discussion
    1. *How often do we use The Law to entrap other people?*

2. What are the things in our life that prevent us from sowing pardon where there is injury?

3. Was there a time when you had forgiven someone even though everyone around you advised you not to pardon the person?

4. How does it feel to forgive another person? How does it feel to be forgiven?

Sowing Unity

As we continue reciting the second movement, I wonder, how can we provide unity where there is discord? The Prayer of St. Francis offers us another way, a better way, a more authentic way. The root of this prayer seeks to build genuine unity amid discord, but we can only receive unity by our willingness to listen to one another, to forgive one another, and to love one another.

I am always amazed on Inauguration Day. Often the president, after being sworn in, delivers a speech calling for unity and renewal, encouraging "both sides" to work together for the common good, and offering hope that together, the next four years can prove prosperous. Unfortunately, within days, discord takes over the call to union. Our culture of division seems to prevail over the call to unity. Therefore, how can we overcome the perils of discord and sow union?

As Christians, we need to realize that the Gospel transcends any political ideology or governmental constitution. The ways of humankind are not the ways of God. As a result, we must strive to sow union wherever we live, work, and worship. The counter action to debate is dialogue. The counter action to false testimony is living into the authentic self as designed by God. The counter action to dehumanization of people is acknowledging their inherent Divine Nature, for we are all made in God's image. Even though it may seem like an uphill battle, we can prevail over discord by constantly sowing union.

Perhaps reflecting on the opening of Psalm forty-two, we may realize the only way to sow union where there is discord is by thirsting for God:

"As a deer longs for flowing streams,/ so my soul longs for you, O God./ My soul thirsts for God,/ for the living God./ When shall I come and behold/ the face of God?"

Perhaps, as "a deer longs for flowing streams," we too must long for the flowing stream that flows from the love of God, just like the blood and water flowing from Jesus' side after he is pierced. As Christ hung on the cross, he saved the world and refused to condemn it. His sacrifice sowed union. He offered himself so that all people could be saved from sin through him. No discord just union. His resurrection brought forth more union as the apostles came together to realize that Christ is known for the breaking of the bread. Today, we still come together and become united by the breaking of the bread and come to know Christ. We come to know Christ in community, together, with one another. We are then called to deliver Christ to the wider community.

We must respond to discord not by becoming belligerent and argumentative but by listening and entering into dialogue – a dialogue in which we are not looking to win a debate but to engage the other person with love and understanding, with openness and hospitality, with sensitivity and empathy. We cannot position ourselves as adversaries or enemies. We need to position ourselves as advocates of righteousness and lovers of our enemies. Sometimes we may need to turn the other cheek. Sometimes we may need to shake the dust from our feet. Regardless, in order to achieve union, we must always keep God in the center of all of our relationships by *respecting the individual dignity of every human being.*

The Lord's prayer aims to remind us of unity over discord when we say, "Your kingdom come. Your will be done on earth as in heaven." If we can bring about God's will here on earth as it exists in heaven, then we will nurture union of those two domains, bringing the alignment of heaven and earth into focus so that we become – not the architects – but the builders of God's kingdom here on earth.

I remember in one community where I worked, I received input from the African American constituents, which was a minority of the community, that the hymn, "Lift Every Voice and Sing," was the Black National Anthem. As a result, they felt uncomfortable because they were taught to stand any time it was performed and in this community people didn't stand. As the spiritual leader, I explained to the assembly that from this point forward any time the hymn was performed at our gathering, we would stand. I explained that the hymn is the Black National Anthem. As with all national anthems, people stand to show respect. Also, we would stand from "this day forward" in order that we may also stand in solidarity with our Black brothers and sisters. I thought my explanation was sufficient. However, I received a number of phone calls questioning my decisions. The comments varied from "Isn't this divisive?" to "How can a race have a national anthem?" to "If we stand for the Black National Anthem, we are causing more division." The statements for the most part rolled off my back and I simply listened in a pastoral capacity. However, the last statement, I responded, "I believe that by standing and showing solidarity for our Black neighbors that we are bringing people together by our show of respect." It always amazes me that when we give to other people what we have – whether it is privilege or respect, critics cry "Division," which only sows more discord.

In the end, when I teach the Cain and Abel story and we arrive at Cain's famous question, "Am I my brother's keeper?" I ask the students, "Since God doesn't directly answer the question, what is God's implied response?"

The students always say, "Yes, we are expected to be our brother's keeper." I then add, "In this story of sibling rivalry, the authors present a conflict of our own interest – self versus other. So, if we are indeed our brother's keeper, we are expected to continue to read The Bible with that in mind. In matter of fact, the rest of scriptures explains how we are to be our brother's keeper. In addition, the definition of brother is expanded to the orphan, widow, and stranger in our midst and ultimately to neighbor. By the time we arrive at the ministry of Jesus, Jesus expands the definition of neighbor to make it universal and inclusive.

Paul, when he wrote to the Galatians, understood this reality. He instructed the Galatians that Christ has become the unifying force in our lives of faith. We inherit the promise of Abraham through the faith of Christ, and, as a result, we are united by him not through doctrine or dogma but by the grace of his faith. Therefore, "There is no longer Jew or Greek, there is no longer slave or free, there is no longer male and female; for all of you are one in Christ Jesus. And if you belong to Christ, then you are Abraham's offspring, heirs according to the promise."

God invites us into unity not through our own work but through the one faith of Jesus Christ whose work on our behalf offers all of us the same salvation. Our call to sow unity where there is discord becomes the essential measure of our faith.

Scriptural Application: Ephesians 4

In the Letter to the Ephesians, the author paints the cosmic reality of God while emphasizing the need to promote "the body's [community] growth in building itself up in love." The letter instructs the Ephesians to carry out specific behaviors that will solidify their fundamental unity. The Letter states:

I therefore, the prisoner in the Lord, beg you to lead a life worthy of the calling to which you have been called, with all humility and gentleness, with patience, bearing with one another in love, making every effort to maintain the unity of the Spirit in the bond of peace. There is one body and one Spirit, just as you were called to the one hope of your calling, one Lord, one faith, one baptism, [6]one God and Father of all, who is above all and through all and in all (Ephesians 4: 1 – 6).

The implication rests on the fact that God calls us "to lead a life worthy of the calling" in which we embrace "all humility and gentleness" with regards to our neighbor. Our "humility and gentleness" must stand on the foundation of our "patience" which will bear "one another in love" and lead us "to maintain the unity of the Spirit in the bond of peace." As people of God, we become initiated through baptism to one body or one community, and the ever-expanding neighborhood where all are welcomed and embraced with the radical hospitality of the love of God. If anything, we are united by one baptism because there is only one baptism, through which God invites us into a faith where we "respect the individual dignity of every human being." That is the foundation of our baptismal covenant. Therefore, we engage in "the one hope of [our] calling to the one God and father of all."

In essence, our relationships with one another can trace its source back to God, the creator of heaven and earth. Or in other words, our radical beginning.

Questions for Further Discussion
1. To what extent are you willing to call out the need to sow unity where there is discord?
2. How can we transcend our individual insecurities in order to sow union?
3. What do we need to surrender in order to achieve unity?
4. What blind spots do we have to sowing unity where there is discord?

Sowing Hope
The prayer points out how the world needs hope, faith, and joy. As a result, we need to become champions of hope rather than promoters of despair. I can illustrate this point with two contrasting stories. First, I remember a time in my youth when my brother and I were driving to the Pocono Mountains in Pennsylvania. My brother, who drove, noticed the gas gauge was nearing empty. I had reminded him how I warned him that we should have filled the tank before we departed our house in Philadelphia. I also reminded him of how he dismissed my warning. Now we were about fifty miles from the next gas station, and he believed in his heart that we would make it. He became the champion of hope. I explained we will never make it. He called me "the prophet of doom" and explained, "Focusing on the negative won't help our situation." I countered with, "If you would have just listened to me before we left, we would not be in this situation."

He emphasized, "We will make it to the gas station before

we run out of gas."

I retorted, "We won't." In the end, we made it to the gas station and my brother enjoyed the last laugh, calling me the prophet of doom, or in other words, the promoter of despair.

A second story reminds me of how I leaned heavy on hope in a situation that was headed for great despair and even death. On a medical trip to Haiti, I leaned on hope during one of the longest nights in my life.

I was leading a team of medical professionals, students, and teachers to the Central Plateau of Haiti in a tiny remote village named Cerca, which sat high in the mountains, four hours from the closest road. The people of Cerca had no access to water, plumbing or electricity. We knew we had stepped out of our comfort zone. I had warned the team of the harsh conditions and explained that we would live as they lived during our visit. Everyone embraced the experience.

After the first eight-hour shift of the medical clinic, one of the nurses asked if she could rest. As she rested, she became ill. She started to vomit and lose fluids. She was highly dehydrated but worse, she was most likely suffering from hyponatremia. Earlier, she was so concerned about becoming hydrated that she took in more water than her body cold absorb. As a result, her body passed the excess liquid and along with it, her electrolytes. She became despondent. She needed an IV to restore her electrolytes. Unfortunately, we did not have the supplies that she needed. As the leader of the team, I had to make a decision between two choices: Stay and hope she recovers on her own or take her down the mountain in the pitch dark of night and risk getting lost or injuring more people. I consulted the other two doctors who were with us. They agreed, *"If she doesn't get off the mountain and to a hospital, she will die."* The decision was made. I explained the situation to my counterpart, Pere Jeannot, and he said, "It is too dangerous to go down the mountain at night."

I responded, "Let me have a horse and a guide because I am leaving with our team member." Since he understood the severity of the situation, he made an announcement in Haitian Creole to the people who came for the medical clinic. I am not sure what he said. Nevertheless, six strong young Haitian men stepped forward. Two others came forward with a makeshift stretcher. A group of women approached me and had me take them to the ailing medical worker. They prayed over her before we put her on the stretcher and we began a long journey into the night.

I walked beside her and tried to keep her focused on the positive. "We've got this. You are going to make it." One of the doctors from our team came with us. She pulled me aside and said, "This doesn't look good. I'm not sure she will make it. Four hours is a long time."

I added, "And we have a forty five minute drive to the hospital in Mirebalais."

She responded, "Be prepared for the worst."

With that sense of despair, I prayed. I kept a positive attitude and leaned on hope. As we descended the mountain, she took a turn for the worse and had a convulsion. Things looked grim. She went in and out of consciousness. She asked who was going to take care of her girls. She knew she was dying. I responded, "You will take care of your daughters."

The six Haitian men who stepped forward on the mountain had volunteered to carry her down the mountain. They took turns and moved rather rapidly. I don't think on any of the trips, we moved so fast as a group. There was a river crossing, and when we arrived at the river at around two in the morning, I was shocked that we had made it there so soon. I kept praying as we boarded the dug-out canoes and started across the river. The darkness matched the despair that was prevalent. I kept leaning on hope. I said to the doctor who earlier had said that things didn't look good, "We will come out of this. I just know it."

She responded, "I hope so."

We finally made it to the road and put our colleague in the ambulance and headed to Mirebalais. While on the ambulance, she had two more seizures. Now we were concerned about brain bleeds. At this point, she needed more than IV fluids. She needed a CAT Scan. When we arrived at the hospital in Mirebalais, things looked grim. No doctor was present. We had some Haitian medical students who did their best, but due to our poor language skills, we failed to communicate what was wrong with Nancy. They did the best they could. At this time, I called International SOS to schedule a medical helicopter to take us to Port-Au-Prince where we would transfer our colleague to a medical jet that would take her to Miami so she could receive the medical treatment she needed. I clung to hope. I felt the hope and it was palpable. Hours passed.

Finally, the helicopter landed at the hospital, and it took her to Port-Au-Prince where she was placed on a medical jet and flown to Miami. I hoped and prayed. She made a full recovery and is now living a happy, healthy and productive life. Hope in this case overcame despair.

The two previous stories present our option of choosing despair or hope. As prophets of doom, we forecast a bleak outcome no matter the circumstance. As beacons of hope, we project the possibilities and mysteries of good outcomes even in the face of great odds. Therefore, as Christians, Christ calls us to a life of hope not only for the here and now, but for eternal life.

Scriptural Application: Romans 5: 1 -5

One could argue that Paul possesses more hope than any other biblical figure. He suffered shipwrecks, floggings, and imprisonment. Nothing deterred him from spreading the Gospel. He believed deeply in his heart that God would transform his suffering just as God transformed Jesus' suffering. This is the hope through which he delivered the gospel. In his letter to the Romans, Paul best explains the truth of Christian hope. He states,

"Therefore, since we are justified by faith, we have peace with God through our Lord Jesus Christ, through whom we have obtained access to this grace in which we stand; and we boast in our hope of sharing the glory of God. And not only that, but we also boast in our sufferings, knowing that suffering produces endurance, and endurance produces character, and character produces hope, and hope does not disappoint us, because God's love has been poured into our hearts through the Holy Spirit that has been given to us" (Romans 5: 1 – 5)

Perhaps this section of Paul's letter provides a remarkable parallel to the Prayer of St. Francis. This statement by Paul contains all of the elements of the prayer. However, we need to examine this text more closely. First, Paul intends to travel to Spain and will stop in Rome before he continues his journey "to the ends of the earth." He cannot foretell the future, and I am sure he experiences some fear, doubt, and anxiety about the next steps of his ministry. However, by this point, he had suffered many setbacks and he believes he can trust God. Therefore, he lives a life, centered on God in Christ with the hope of the resurrection.

Paul knew all would be glorified through the faith of Christ. He also knew that if he delivered the gospel message to the ends of the earth, then everyone would enjoy eternal life and be saved. Second, he writes to a divided community. He attempts to explain due to "us who believe in him who raised Jesus our Lord from the death, who was handed over to death for our trespasses and was raised for our justification" that we, whether gentile or Jew, are united by the faith of Christ. Paul advances the hope that those two communities will resolve their differences and look to the one element that unites them – the redemption and salvation offered by Christ. Third, this division may sow the seeds of hope in that if they could overcome their differences because "we are justified by faith [and] we have peace with God through our Lord Jesus Christ." Christ provides a gate through which we can walk together, leaving our differences behind, and become united "to this grace in which we stand." We, too, are called to live in this hope. Furthermore, where there is despair we must sow hope, and as Christians, "we boast in our hope of sharing the glory of God." Afterall, the glory of God lasts forever. Human glory – those materials things which we glorify – fades. Once we realize that we share in the glory of God, then we can boast in all things that lead us to God. We can boast in our suffering because it will lead to endurance. Our endurance can come in any form. For example, we may have to endure everything, from loss of family to loss of income, from loss of health to loss of stature. Whatever the loss, if we focus on "sharing the glory of God," then our suffering will help us build endurance which leads to character. Ultimately, our character, which is built upon our core values, will produce hope. Once we possess hope, then no disappointment can bring about despair because by that point, we believe "God's love has been poured in our hearts through the Holy Spirit." In closing, it is only through our faith in the grace of God that we can sow hope amid despair. As people who carry this hope, we believe we can bring healing to our broken world. We live into this hope that everything is resurrectable and everything can enter into God's glory. Yes, *hope does not disappoint.*

Questions for Further Discussion
    1. Explain a time when you faced a situation of despair and clung to hope. How did you feel? Where was it? Who was with you? How did you live into this hope?
    2. Today, what is the source of your hope?
    3. Where do you see despair?
    4. As Christians, how can we become beacons of hope?

Sowing Faith

We need to become advocates of faith rather than spreaders of doubt. This reality leaves us as sowers of faith in all that we do. In order to advance to this place in our lives, we need to surrender control. I once had a colleague explain to me that conventional thinking leaves us holding onto a reality that doubt is the opposite of faith. Perhaps, faith and doubt claim the opposite sides of the same coin. She went on to explain that control is the opposite of faith. At first, this caused me to scratch my head until I became willing to reorient my thinking.

In my life, all the times that I lacked faith in God resulted from my inability to control a situation. Those situations in my life, when I blamed God for failing me, circled around my inability to obtain something I had desired. I remember one time when I worked with a student who suffered from depression. This was in the early 1990's and long before I had any training in therapy and counseling. I made the mistake of trying to "fix" her. I thought that if I could control her behavior, then I would motivate her. The more she spiraled out of control, the more I tried to "fix" her. As a result, the more I tried to "fix" her, the more she pushed me away. I saw that she was a talented student, and I had assessed that she was throwing away an excellent opportunity. To counterbalance her self-destructive behavior, I created rigid guidelines for her. For example, she needed to check in with me throughout the school day, so I could make sure she wasn't using drugs, to ensure that she was adhering to the dress code, and to make sure she was where she was supposed to be. When she refused to follow my rules, I became angry and tried to install a new set of rules. Our relationship began to crumble. Each time I created rigid rules that she either refused or wasn't able to follow, I sowed more seeds of doubt. She didn't have faith that I had her best interest at heart. The reverse was true, too. I didn't have faith that she was trying to improve her situation. As doubt mounted, I tried more attempts to control her behavior. It only resulted in doubt.

My refusal to believe that I was incapable of "fixing" this student's problems led me to not rely on any assistance I needed. For example, we had mental health experts who were capable of handling the issues surrounding this promising student. However, my need to control the situation and my choice not to have faith in them only deepened the pain and suffering this student was enduring.

Sadly, the school expelled her, which reflected not only her unwillingness to comply with the rules and regulations but also my inability to have faith in other people who could have helped us both. There is a saying I once heard a wise man share with me, "Either make a difference or make room." This was a situation where my faith should have made room for someone else to step in to make a difference for this student. In the end, I have come to the realization that indeed, control is the opposite of faith. Control only sows seeds of doubt.

Scriptural Application God reckons his faith as righteous (Genesis 15: 1 – 6)

Scripture contains many stories of faith from Moses to Ruth, from Mary to Stephen. However, I keep returning to Abraham and the great faith he put into God's promise. Abraham believed God when in all actuality the evidence was overwhelmingly against the odds of Abraham and Sarah bearing a child. However, Abraham often went up against the odds. He left home at God's request and never needed to know the destination. He arrived at the "land God showed him" and he faced the harsh reality of a famine. He relocated to Egypt. In essence, Abraham never tried to control the situation to which God led him. He simply believed in God's providence. He valued God's providence more than he valued controlling his own destiny. Therefore, on that dark, starry night, when he lamented to God, "You have given me no offspring, and so a slave born in my house is to be my heir." He remained open to the possibilities of God. The word of the Lord came to him, "Look toward heaven and count the stars, if you are able to count them....So shall your descendants be." Abraham heard the word and believed. He knew that he had no control over the reality of procreation. He was old. Sarah was old. They were both beyond the window of opportunity to have children. He surrendered control and put his faith in God. God "reckoned [his faith] to him as righteousness." Abraham teaches all of us that it is better to sow seeds of faith rather than exacting control over a situation.

If we look closely at Abraham, God considers him righteous long before Abraham does anything. For example, God considers him righteous before he circumcises himself, his sons, and his male servants. God considers him righteous long before Abraham demonstrates his willingness to follow God's command to sacrifice Isaac. Paul points this out in his letter to the Romans. Faith becomes the foundation upon which the promise rests. We, as a result of this faith, receive the promise, too. The question becomes, "How do we respond to this faith? Do we put all of our faith in God and follow the Great Command to love God with all our heart, all our soul, and all our strength?" Our faith calls us to direct all of our intentions to God. Our faith demands that we put God at the center of our lives. Therefore, our actions fulfill our prayers, and our prayers shape our actions. Jesus draws us toward God in all that we do. We cannot live into a check box religion: Attended church, check. Made a charitable donation, check. Prayed for the sick, check. We must resist doing good and then moving forward as though there were no connections between our Christian "actions" and our daily living. As William Law[3] says, "If we are to follow Christ, then it must be our common way of spending every day."

Questions for Further Discussion:
    1. What does true faith look like?
    2. As Christians, how are we called into faith?
    3. In our long tradition, who provides the best examples of faithfulness to follow?
    4. In our daily lives, where must we surrender control in order to live into our faith?

Sowing Light
    We need to become beacons of light rather than sponsors of

---

[3] A Serious Call to a Devout and Holy Life by William Law

darkness. Darkness is a human paradox. On one hand, we fear the darkness. For example, walking along the ocean on a moonless night can become quite overwhelming. If one begins to imagine what it would be like to be stranded in the deep ocean, miles from shore, on a small raft, fear shoots through the body. Also, I remember as a child, I was comforted always seeing a sliver of light shining in my bedroom at night, so I could fall asleep without the distractions of my imagination conjuring up monsters and beasts and bad guys storming my bed. On the other hand, as humans, we cling to the darkness. We intentionally hide in the darkness of our mind in order to conceal our sins, our flaws, and our blind spots. We remain in the darkness to avoid exposure.

Perhaps, this dichotomy of light and darkness becomes most evident in the tension we have between noise and silence. We love noise. We are able to hide our true selves in the clutter of our lives – the music in our ear buds, the television in the background, the mental distractions of what we need to do tomorrow and what we failed to do yesterday. I equate the darkness with the noise of our lives because both keep us from discovering who we are and who God is. Perhaps, this reality contributes to the mental health epidemic plaguing America. We hide behind the noise and conceal our true selves in the darkness. We fear being exposed to ourselves and to others. Therefore, entering silence, which ultimately leads to light, intimidates us and terrifies us. However, if we enter the silence which leads to the light, then we will become liberated from all of the darkness and noise that ultimately entraps our true selves.

In our competitive culture, we constantly compare ourselves to others. We look outward to find ourselves. This also reflects how we try to find God. We measure our self-worth by our net worth or by our awards and accolades or by the square footage of our houses or the model of the cars that we drive. These material things just conceal who we truly are and make us fall deeper into the darkness and the clutter of our minds. We become lost. We fall away from the reality of what the light truly reveals, which is our goodness, our desire to become one with God, our need to serve one another, and our radical beginning, or the root of our true self fully aligned with the Divine Image. However, these things which can lead us into the light also can conceal us in the darkness. Our motivation to develop goodness or our desire to become one with God, and our need to serve one another can lead us to self-righteousness. Our self-righteousness draws us into the darkness where we cling to the letter of the Law and fail to embrace the spirit of Law. Ultimately, we need to reflect and pray on our ministry and vocation and ask, "Why do we do the things we do? How do these things make us beacons of light as opposed to sponsors of darkness?" The following story may give some insight into this tension between the light and the darkness.

Back in the early 1980's when I was in a religious order, I was involved in opening a soup kitchen in Allentown, Pennsylvania. In order to learn how to run and operate a soup kitchen, I joined the staff of St. Francis Inn, which sits beneath the Market Frankford El in the Kensington section of Philadelphia.

Each day, hundreds of people came to the soup kitchen for their meals. They would start lining up in the shadow of the Market Frankford El and wait. In addition to offering meals, we would offer social services and take care of minor injuries, cuts and bruises. Young teenage mothers came to us needing baby food and diapers, which we gladly provided, when we had them, and gladly accepted their insults when we didn't have the items in our pantry.

I have to admit that the time I spent at St. Francis Inn was like no other. It was like no other because, as a young man who had joined a religious order, I became quickly disillusioned with the Church.

I entered what one would call a spiritual desert. I would pray and felt nothing. I felt no presence of God in any part of my life. I never doubted that God existed, but I felt abandoned and isolated.

I have to admit that it was the only time in my life that I ever felt lonely. In essence, I was lost in the darkness.

However, one Saturday in the heat of the summer I was in the courtyard of St. Francis Inn. It was a paved area where a house once stood. It was enclosed by a chain-linked fence. It served as a waiting area for people who desired to receive a meal. In-between meals, kids would play wall ball or just hang out. Some of the homeless men would lean against the fence and smoke cigarettes and drink bottles of beer hidden in brown paper bags.

Each day, one of the staff members would be assigned to station the area to keep peace among the people who gathered there. This one particular Saturday, when I was on duty, the courtyard was empty. It was extremely hot and humid.

The soup kitchen welcomed many regulars to our tables and some of the regulars were characters that had reputations for one thing or another. This Saturday, one of them, Joe, entered the courtyard staggering drunk and somewhat incoherent. He demanded clean socks. I invited him to sit down on one of the folder chairs we had lined up against the wall. He sat and slumped in the chair, complaining that his feet hurt. I went inside to find some clean socks and Brother Tom, one of the Franciscans, told me where they were.

He asked, "Who are they for?"

I told him, and he said, "You will need to clean his feet." I looked at him. Actually, I gave him a dirty look.

"You need water, soap, and a towel," he added. I retrieved everything I needed.

At that point, I wished I wasn't the one on duty. I knew Joe. I also knew that he was one of the most ungrateful people we served. He appreciated nothing; whether it was feeding him, taking him to the hospital, or providing him with clothes, he always had a complaint. In addition, I had never met him when he was sober. So, I went out to the courtyard and the El rumbled overhead and Joe looked up and rumbled back at the El.

"I have your socks, Joe."

"Who are you?" He demanded.

"Tim," I answered.

"Are you one of the brothers?"

"No. I am a volunteer. I belong to another religious order."

"I want one of the brothers."

"Sorry, Joe," I responded sarcastically. "I am all that you have."

He grumbled and said, "Take off my shoes." I removed his shoes and was hit with the worst foot odor I had ever smelled. His socks were stuck to his feet and when I took them off, the odor became even more foul. I was doing everything I could do not to gag.

"Be careful," he snapped.

"Your feet are a mess, Joe."

"No kidding. Any moron can see that," he barked.

His feet were cracked and bloodied. I put the towel in the bucket and rung it out over both of his feet. The dirt and blood mingled as the water dripped off his feet. All of a sudden, John's

Gospel came alive for me right there in the courtyard in one of the poorest sections of Philadelphia with one of the most ungrateful human beings I had ever met. I felt a certain calm as if I was being ushered from a place of upheaval to a place of serenity. I couldn't comprehend the change in my attitude toward Joe, but the frost seemed to melt. He even seemed to relax.

I washed his feet and dried them. I went back inside, found some powder and sprinkled it on his instep and between his toes. All of a sudden, for the first time in a long time, I felt the presence of God right there on Kensington Avenue as the El rattled above our heads as it passed from one stop to another. Joe quieted down in the echoes of the El train as it decrescendo-ed out of earshot. The courtyard was quiet and I looked at Joe as I never looked at him before. I saw more than a belligerent drunk. I saw more than a homeless man. I saw more than an ungrateful person. I felt connected to him as if the image of God in him reached out and embraced the image of God in me. At that moment – I felt the transformational power of the Gospel and understood intuitively the act of Jesus when he washed the feet of the disciples.

After suffering in the spiritual desert for quite some time as a young man, I came out of that wilderness in the most unsuspecting context – not in some grand cathedral with the most glorious liturgy, but in a small concrete courtyard outside of a soup kitchen beneath the Market-Frankford El. I finally felt the presence of God. I felt the warmth of God's light. I was immersed in the light that the darkness could not overtake.

In the portrayal of the Foot Washing in Johns' Gospel, we see Jesus performing a humble act not simply as a symbolic act. According to Brendan Byrne[4] in his book, *Life Abounding*, the foot washing is an expression of the radical reversal of social

---

[4] *Life Abounding* by Brendan Byrne

status. It lives as an extraordinary display of self-sacrificing love that will culminate in the crucifixion. Jesus washes the apostles' feet in order that they, the Apostles, will extend this self-sacrificing love in mutual service to one another and to the world. "The foot washing and the cross mutually illuminate each other as the supreme revelation of divine love expressed as service to others," writes Byrne.

If I am honest, on that Saturday morning in the early 1980's, the last thing I wanted to do was wash Joe's feet. At that moment, I wanted to be anywhere but there. He resented us even though we served all of his needs. I resented him for his lack of gratitude. I felt no purpose in helping this man who had so many times inflicted harm on himself either through drinking or picking fights with the wrong people. I was in a period where my prayer and spiritual life were unfulfilling.

As I had mentioned earlier, I was lost in a spiritual desert. Joe was lost in his own turmoil. And here, God brings Joe and me together on this one Saturday morning in the heat of summer, and invites two people to transcend their own personal struggles in order to walk in the light of Christ. I put the clean socks on Joe's feet. I tied his shoes. He said as a clear as day, "Thank you, Tim."

The El rumbled overhead, and I said, "No, Joe. Thank you."

This story illustrates the refusal for each person, Joe and me, to leave the darkness of their own struggles, their own inner pain in order to enter the light of God's grace and love. Oddly enough, Joe, who I despised, became my beacon of light. He pointed me and led me from the darkness of my own spiritual desert and brought me into the realization that we can find the light of Christ within each other and ultimately, deep within ourselves.

Ultimately, to become a beacon of light, we must incorporate contemplation into our prayer life. Our prayer life usually becomes filled with the noise of words, the distractions of our own mind, and the demands of our occupations. We think we must recite this prayer or that prayer. We must read the daily lectionary. We do these things with good intentions and they are good for us. However, they can become the very things that keep us from going inward to the depth of our being, to the center of our suffering. One may ask, why would we want to journey to the center of our being if we are only to end up at the center of our suffering? Good question. However, many of our spiritual sages dating back as far as our tradition goes illustrate for us that the center of our being and our suffering is where we ultimately find God. Christ is at the center of our being. Christ is the "light that entered the darkness, and the darkness could not overtake it." It may take years and one attempt after another to descend to the depths of our depths. However, along that journey, we arrive at stops that provide us glimpses of the light. For example, the light that Joe brought into the interaction could only flourish because he is made in God's image just as I am made in God's image. Our interaction led us both inward.

I was aware of my anger and resentment. I also came to the realization during the encounter of my disillusionment with the Church. Joe forced me to go within. Joe forced me to ask, "Why am I doing this? What is my purpose? Where is Christ in all of this poverty and suffering?" As Joe became more settled in his chair and relaxed about my aid, he became more human to me. My resentment as I dwelled inward decreased. At that moment, Joe helped me to understand that my disillusionment with the Church was not directed at Christ. At that moment, even though I could not align the head of the Church, Christ, with the body of the Church, I felt peace. I sensed that Christ called me beyond the clutter of my life. He summoned be to walk through the darkness toward the light. He wanted me to discover who I truly was in Christ.

When I felt the image of God within Joe reach out and embrace the image of God in me, I understood that it was better to be exposed in the light than to be buried in the darkness. In a sense, that interaction which forced me to go deep within to face my resentment, anger, and disillusionment allowed a shaft of light to burst forth on the scene that originated in the core of my being. The foot washing itself wasn't the "God experience." The light shining deep within the darkness, which the darkness failed to conceal, rose to the surface and revealed our true nature as human beings. Both of us in need of love. Both of us in need of compassion. Both of us in need of God. That Saturday morning, so many years ago, proved that both of us in our own suffering could become beacons of light rather than sponsors of darkness.

Scriptural Application: John 8, The Woman Caught in Adultery

Once again, I must return to the story of the Woman Caught in Adultery. I see a great religious paradox in this episode of John's Gospel. Of course, when Jesus says, "Let anyone among you who is without sin be the first to throw a stone at her," he hits an ironic bull's eye. However, I see the paradox long before Jesus' memorable statement. The paradox lies in the opening scene. Jesus is teaching in the Temple precinct and many people come to listen. The scribes and pharisees bring a woman to him who had been caught in the act of adultery. In a sense, they take her from the darkness of sin and expose it in the light. With the guilt of her sin, she stands before the crowd and Jesus in her own vulnerability. She can't say much on her own behalf. She is made to stand there, "before all of them."

The scribes and Pharisees bring her out of the darkness and into the light for their own nefarious motives, to trap Jesus in an attempt to bring "some charge against him." Jesus bends down and begins to write "with his finger in the sand." In a sense, Jesus descends to the depths of the earth and as some ancient text contains, he wrote out the sins of each person in the crowd who was ready to stone the woman. At that moment, Jesus brings them out of their own darkness and invites them into the light, the light that reveals who they truly are as people. In essence, Jesus makes them vulnerable before God just as the woman is vulnerable before God. He offers them an opportunity to gain a radical beginning by meeting their own sins face to face right there in the dirt. Jesus understands that all of them are suffering from sin and right below the surface of those sins is the place where they can meet God and as a result find who they truly are meant to be.

After all, this is the same dirt though which God created Adam and breathed the spirit of life into him. Jesus gives the angry, manipulative crowd the same opportunity to receive the spirit of God by acknowledging their sins and receiving forgiveness through the grace of God. Jesus' great statement, "Let anyone among you who is without sin be the first to throw a stone at her" offers a gift of redemption to all present. At that moment all of them stand in the light. They at least for that moment had escaped the darkness. If they had been willing to take ownership their own sins just as they wanted the woman to take ownership her own sins, then they would have found new life in Christ, a radical beginning where they could embrace humility which is the foundation of all virtues and lived lives to the glory of God. However, they found more security in the cover of darkness instead of embracing the freedom in the assurance of light.

The great paradox lies in the fact that Jesus invites them into the light and they refuse, dropping their stones but clinging to the Letter of the Law. They fail to see how the light will lead them to the true Spirit of the Law. They fail to see that Jesus is "the light of the world" and "whoever follows [him] will never walk in darkness but will have the light of life."

Of all the people who had been present, the woman remains alone standing before Jesus. I imagine she still feels vulnerable and exposed. Perhaps shame calls her back to the darkness, but she stands firm in her vulnerability and remains before Jesus waiting, perhaps waiting for his final judgment. However, as readers, we hear the echo of John 3, "For God so loved the world that he gave his only son, so that everyone who believes in him may not perish but may have eternal life." The woman stands on the precipice of this reality, and the echo of John 3 continues, "Indeed, God did not send the Son into the world to condemn the world, but in order that the world might be saved through him." Therefore, Jesus did not write the sins of the scribes and Pharisees to condemn them but to invite them into the saving embrace of God. In reality, they chose sin over God and left the scene to return to the darkness. God remained within their grasp beyond the scribble in the sand. They only needed to go beyond the surface. What a missed opportunity. They receded into the darkness of their sins instead of taking hold of the light into which they stepped.

The woman stands before Jesus becoming a beacon of the light rather than a sponsor of the darkness and simply relies on Jesus' grace. Jesus stands up and asks rhetorically, "Woman, where are they? Has no one condemned you?" She simply responds, "No one, sir."

Jesus responds, "Neither do I."

However, somehow as readers, we realize that he was never going to condemn her. We know that forgiveness is at hand and he offers it to her freely and abundantly and says, "Go your way, and from now on do not sin again." In other words, Jesus instructs her to continue walking in the light. In the end, she is the beacon of the light among the self-righteous sponsors of the darkness.

Questions for Further Discussion

1. How do we cling to the darkness?
2. Who shows us the light and how does this revelation provide us with a radical beginning?
3. How does acknowledging and owning our sin lead us into the light of grace and redemption?
4. How can we be beacons of the light as opposed to the sponsors of darkness?

Sowing Joy

We need to infiltrate joy into the lives of those who suffer sorrow. The idea of spreading joy seems more Pollyanna than virtuous. Is joy a virtue? I know from experience a number of people who have sucked joy out of a room and made everyone feel miserable. From this view, I believe joy is a virtue. I see it as a virtue because Joy lifts other people up. Joy brings out the best of others. In contrast, misery brings out the worst in others. I am sure we all have known people who exhibit both the virtue of joy and the vice of misery.

Before moving forward, let's define joy by defining what it is not. Joy is not happiness. Happiness comes from extrinsic rewards. We find happiness in a job promotion only to realize that this job doesn't bring the satisfaction we believed. We find happiness in the latest iPhone only to realize it has many limits compared to the next model. We find happiness in our favorite desert only to realize a little bit goes a long way, and we wish we had not eaten it.

We have met people who on the surface seem like good people. However, once we scratch beyond the surface, we find them to be flares of sorrow. Once, I had a colleague who didn't know any joy. Let's call her Lapenn. She embraced the sorrow of the world. She allowed her own sorrow to play over and over in her mind like an endless loop of video. She often projected her sorrow and pain onto others.

She worked with small children. They could not bring her joy. She saw them as "spoiled kids" and projected her feelings of them onto their parents. She built boundaries and walls around her and between herself and others. In addition, she made life difficult for her colleagues. She presented her position as her way or the highway. One time, when a four-year-old child took a crayon from her desk, she descended upon the child like a hawk on a fieldhouse. "Who said you could take that crayon from my desk?"

The volume in which she spoke made the child jump. The child was startled, and her fear was evident by how she clutched the crayon. The child stood on the verge of tears, tears welling up in her eyes, her knees shaking, and her lips twitching. Lapenn continued her tirade, "Who do you think you are to take something from my desk without asking? How dare you invade my private space!" She turned red and a thick vein protruded from her neck. Her colleagues stood in shock. No one knew what to do. In a sense, they couldn't believe that a four-year-old student taking a crayon from a desk would illicit such an unreasonable response. Lapenn went on for another minute or two and finally asked, "Why did you need that crayon? Why is it so important?"

The child found a way to transcend her tears and answered, "I wanted this crayon because it was purple, and I wanted to draw you a flower using your favorite color."

Later, when her colleagues tried to reason with Lapenn, she directed a short tirade toward them about being "enablers" and for failing to be professional since they were taking the child's side. "If you were truly interested in the moral development of these kids, you would hold them accountable for stealing," Lapenn attacked. Somewhat bewildered, one of them commented, "It's hardly stealing. The crayon and your desk are part of our classroom."

"You prove my point," Lapenn snapped. She turned on her heels and left the classroom.

This four-year-old child tried to sow joy where there was sorrow by making a drawing for her teacher using the teacher's favorite color. The instinct of the student went to the heart of this movement of the prayer – where there was sadness, she wanted to sow joy. Perhaps, the child (and I think most children possess this ability) perceived the sadness lodged deep within Lapenn. I never met a four-year-old who didn't want to sow joy. I think that is what Jesus meant when he said, "If we want to enter the kingdom of heaven, then we must become like a child." Children are beacons of joy. They find joy in simple pleasures from blowing the seeds of a dandelion to licking the cake batter of a bowl, from jumping in puddles to drawing rainbows. They see the source of joy almost everywhere. As a matter of fact, if you ever experience a bad day, visit a Pre-Kindergarten classroom anywhere in the country and you will leave feeling better about yourself and about the world. Let's be childlike and sow joy where there is sorrow.

I've learned in my long career as an educator not to dismiss the wisdom and insights of a child, especially children under six years old. They come to us unjaded and pure in their thoughts. I believe the Holy Spirit truly speaks through them. As a result, they sow joy pretty much wherever they go. For instance, I remember one time I was leading a religion class that focused on the nature of God. Let me first note, on one level, the abstract nature of this conversation may well be beyond the four-year-old's cognitive ability. However, most four-year-olds, when it comes to abstract ideas, intuitively know not to rely on intellect. They find comfort in mystery. As a result, they approach "these abstract ideas" with open hearts. Therefore, wisdom flows through them like running water.

When I had asked the students who God was, I received many answers. One student, Isla, said, "God is light. We all have light within our hearts. So, God must also be in our hearts." I inquired what that means for us as people if God is within our hearts. Another student, Stephen, burst out, "Well, if God is in your heart and Isla's heart and my heart, we need to be nice to each other." The simplicity of seeing God in that manner provides a wonderful window into true joy. I have discovered through the eyes of children that simplicity leads to joy. On one hand, adults tend to complicate ideas. Adults tend to outthink their own notion of what God is or what God can be for them in their daily lives. They comment internally on all they think about. They allow their minds to become cluttered with self-loathing or self-aggrandizement, with comparing our possessions to other people's possessions, and with thinking what needs to be done next to thinking what we failed to do yesterday. All of these thoughts complicate our lives and lead us to regret and sorrow. On the other hand, children tend to think in this present moment. They enjoy playing when they are playing. They enjoy singing when they are singing. The enjoy a clutter-free mind to see things as they are. For example, purple is a beautiful color. It can be used to draw a flower or to dress a princess. Children appreciate the magic of a rainbow and the design of a bird's nest without filtering their thoughts through a self-criticizing lens. I have never heard a child say of her own thought, "Gee, that was a silly idea." Children tend not to complicate things because they realize the world before them presents opportunities to explore, to inquire, and to discover things not only about the world itself but about themselves and others. As a result, they sow joy and reap joy. What a beautiful harvest!

Scriptural Application: "I have neither silver or gold..." (Acts 3:6)

The disciples experienced great fear and confusion at the arrest, crucifixion, and death of Jesus. Once Jesus was buried, I am certain they assumed all their hope accompanied Jesus' body to the tomb where it would decay along with the flesh. However, I think it is safe to say that initially, the resurrection of Jesus only confused and bewildered them. For forty days Jesus appeared and reappeared to them. It was not until the final commission and ascension that the disciples understood they were not alone. Jesus promises the advocacy of the Holy Spirit. When the burning tongues descend upon them in the upper room, they receive the joy when each one of them "is filled with the Holy Spirit."

With this joy, they go into the world spreading the Good News in every language and joyfully offer the invitation to salvation and freedom from sin to all people and to every nation. Their joy rests in the reality that Jesus empowers them to go into the world to do the work he gave them to do – forgiving sinners, healing the sick, freeing the captives. With this empowerment by

God, who wouldn't be joyful?

They take their joy and sow it where there is sorrow. I love the story of the healing of the lame beggar. I remember translating this story from the Latin Vulgate when I was an undergrad. The imagery of the man leaping and bounding made me laugh. However, it wasn't a laugh of irony or disbelief. It was more of a laugh that represents the joy of a child who experiences something for the first time.

Peter goes to the temple at the hour of prayer and sees people carrying a lame man and lay him before the Beautiful Gate. This gave the man an opportunity to beg for money. When Peter and John were about to enter the temple, the lame man requested a donation, "expecting to receive something from them." Interestingly, the man would receive much more than a donation. He would be granted the gift of self-agency in which he could walk, become productive, and not rely on handouts. Peter, who "looked intently at him," responded, "I have no silver or gold." I imagine this initial response made the man look beyond Peter and John for the next person from who he could beg. However, Peter continues, "but what I have I give you; in the name of Jesus Christ of Nazareth, stand up and walk." Peter reaches out and takes him by the right hand. I wonder when was the last time this man enjoyed or received human touch. I wonder how many people have passed this man simply dropping a coin into his cup without even making eye contact or uttering a word. To many people, I am sure this man was an object they looked beyond, hoping to avoid any authentic engagement with him. However, Peter looks intently at him and offers him his hand. In essence, Peter offers him human dignity. In addition, when Peter *raises him up*, Peter offers the man a radical beginning, an opportunity to become the person he is meant to be. The man realizes "immediately his feet and ankles were made strong." The man left his station and I imagine his vessel of coins to jump up from the prone position. He "stood and began to walk." However, as "he entered the temple with Peter and John, he was "walking and leaping and praising God." I envision him dancing around the Temple, sowing great joy in all who watched him. People witnessed this man's movements and words as an act of praise – a liturgical dance – and realized this man was "the one who used to sit and ask for alms at the Beautiful Gate of the temple." His joy was palpable and contagious because "they were filled with wonder and amazement at what had happened to him."

Peter and John saw sorrow and planted joy not by giving alms which would work as a temporary fix for the man's troubles or enable the man to continue to live a life of misery and sorrow. They provided him with a life-changing opportunity which afforded him a radical beginning where he could allow the image of God to work in him and praise God, planting joy at the wonders of God's creation.

If we examine this passage from Acts of the Apostles, the man who is healed takes on the joyfulness that only a child could express. He doesn't seem to care about what people may think of him. He doesn't filter his excitement at letting people know what God has done for him. The simplicity of his praise is heartfelt and authentic, very much like that of a child. His sowing of joy where sorrow had been provides a lesson of how our mind, body, and spirit find wholeness when we transcend our own sorrow and accept the joy that comes from God.

Questions for Further Discussion
1. What are the areas in our own life where we need to sow joy?

2. How does a new-found joy become the advent for our radical beginning?

3. How do we find joy in the midst of our own sorrow?

4. How do we use scripture and our prayer life to respond to both the external and internal negativity that invades our lives?

Summary of Second Movement: The Things We Sow

We need to believe that we can rise above and beyond the divisions that exist in our community, in our country, and in our world. Perhaps, the best way we can become united is through empathy. We need to embrace how others see the world while maintaining our personal convictions. This proves a difficult challenge to balance. Perhaps, if we entered into more dialogues than debates, we would learn to empathize with others. See, if we enter our disagreements as dialogue rather than as a debate, then we become more interested in coming to understand the other. If, on the other hand, we enter our disagreements as a debate, then we become lost in the competition of winning and losing. As a result, we oversimplify the other person as an opponent and consequently as an object to defeat or dismiss. When we enter a relationship with the competitive mindset to win and disrupt the other, then we fail to become the neighbor we are meant to be. We keep the person a stranger. We keep the person impersonal. We keep the person at a safe distance.

Consequently, we need to see each person – friend and foe – as our neighbor. We can only do this if we take to heart the need to understand other people's points of view. This requires us to embrace the stranger as our neighbor. We need to transform ourselves and "cut away the hardness of our hearts and be stubborn no longer." We cannot cling to our need to always be right, to be the smartest person in the room, or to be the only one who possesses a good idea. We need to open our hearts to listen, to receive, and to accept others no matter the differences that separate us. We need to possess hearts of ever-expanding mercy where the love of God can grow and flourish and be manifested in our relationships with others.

Scriptural Application: The Sower Went Out Mark 4

As a priest, I have found comfort in the parable of The Sower Went Out. I find comfort because it removes the pressure of harvesting the crop. I simply plant seeds and trust God will take care of the rest. However, the downside to this mindset lies in the reality that I don't always see the fruits of my labors. I have come to realize that I can't force joy although I can plant the seeds of joy. I have come to accept that some people are like the *heavy trodden footpath* or *the rocky ground* or *the field of weeds* where they cannot cultivate the seeds of joy. I am comfortable realizing that I don't have control over the conditions of their life. I hope for the best. Nevertheless, their refusal to accept the seeds of joy doesn't permit one to censure the need to sow seeds of joy. Joy must be sown wherever there is sorrow, darkness, doubt, despair, discord, injury, or hatred.

In the end, we reap what we sow. In addition, we know from nature that sometimes snares and wheat grow together and to uproot the snares endangers the ultimate harvest of the wheat. As Christians, sometimes the cross we must bear requires us to live among the weeds and allow God to take care of those things that are beyond our capabilities. Ultimately, we need to live according to the Golden Rule, which requires us to love, pardon, unify, inspire faith, instill hope, shed light, and sow joy. The challenge remains for us to abide in one another and to abide in God as Christ abides in the Father and the Father in Christ.

Questions for Further Discussion

1. How do you practice sowing the Christian virtues presented in this prayer?

2. What blind spots do we need to uncover in ourselves in order to enable ourselves to sow these virtues?

3. How can we support one another in making communities of sowers?

4. What strategies do we have to avoid becoming discouraged in this work?

Chapter 4

Centering on the Other: The Third Movement

Grant That I May Not Seek So Much

We proceed from the second movement of this short prayer to the third movement, which illustrates how we can become more centered on the needs of others. We do this by consoling, by understanding, and by loving others. We need to become empathetic and see the world from another person's vantage point.

This requires practice, practice, and more practice. However, it first requires a pure heart which embodies the aim of such instruction [rooted in] love that comes from "a pure heart, a good conscience, and sincere faith" (1 Timothy 1:5). Anyone who knows the transformative power of forgiveness understands that at the root of righteous behavior lies a pure heart.

I find that when I have difficulty with another person, I figuratively invite the person into prayer with me. I ask God to help me empathize with the person, to feel compassion for the person, and to forgive the person. The power of prayer molds and shapes my heart to embrace the person. Suddenly, the difficulty I have with the person dissipates like fog at sun rise. However, one time I struggled with a person and simply praying failed to bring the normal remedy. I carried the resentment I had for this person to the point where I became a victim of my own resentment. Fortunately, before ordination I went on retreat. The retreat provided a spiritual director. Since I felt uncomfortable about these feelings I had for this person, I didn't want to move forward until I could escape the darkness of my own feelings. Therefore, I signed up to meet with the spiritual director. I explained to her the situation. I told her how when I invited the person into prayer with me, I could not shake loose the feelings of resentment and anger toward the person. I explained that this surprised me because it always worked.

The spiritual director offered an alternative. She requested that we close our eyes and sit in silence. She would then, after a period of silence elapsed, talk me through a process that might help me shed the shackles of anger and resentment. We sat in silence. I felt comfortable. She then said, "I want you to imagine that you are in a place where you feel safe."

I envisioned that place. She then said, "I want you to draw a large circle on the ground."

I did so.

She advised, "Step into the circle, and now envision that Christ is outside the circle."

I saw the image as clear as day.

"Now ask Christ to join you in the circle."

I did so.

"Now imagine this person is standing outside the circle."

I did so.

"I want you to invite him into the circle."

I did so.

"Are you, Christ, and this person inside the circle?"

"Yes," I responded.

"What do you notice about the person?"

"He's smiling," I responded. "I never see him smiling, but there is pure joy in this circle. I can't begin to describe it." At that moment, the weight of my resentment and anger fell away from me. I felt free. No more did this person feel like a burden. He in that moment became my neighbor. In the presence of Christ, I realized I found the humanity to see within him the Image of God. That made all the difference. This person no longer led me to resentment or anger or judgment. I only wanted to *console, to understand, and to love* him as Christ loved him.

To Console

In essence, the prayer reminds us that we need to focus more on our common humanity where we create room in our hearts to console others. We need to develop compassion, so we are more ready to console rather than focusing on our need to be consoled. St. Francis understood this reality of the gospel and reached out to the untouchables of his day. He embraced – both literally and figuratively – the lepers and the sick, the poor and the destitute, the unwanted and oppressed. He lived to remember those "whom it is easy for us to forget." His humility allowed him to break down barriers that existed between and among people. He saw the gospel as a transcending force that revealed God's light in the world. Bonaventure records Francis' desire to console others, "…in his deep love of humility, [Francis] went among the lepers and remained with them, serving them diligently for the love of God. He washed their feet, bound their wounds, pressing out the corrupt matter, then washed and cleansed them. And having done this, he kissed their wounds with great and marvelous devotion, as one who in brief space was to become an evangelical physician, and the true healer of souls." Francis' willingness to reach out to those whom others rather forget or ignore represents God's command to love your neighbor as yourself.

In our own context, how do we love our neighbor as

ourselves? As we continue to aspire to reach God's will for us through our love for our neighbor, we need to discover what our neighbors need. However, before that we need to know who our neighbors are. According to Jesus, everyone with whom we come in contact becomes our neighbor, which means even our enemy. As we live into that reality, we must learn how to invite others into our sphere and simply ask, "How can I help you?" or "What do you want me to do for you?" These two questions begin our task to console. If we don't know the needs of the other, then we will never be able to console them.

During a short stint as a hospital chaplain, I was tending to a twelve-year-old boy, named Kevin, who was admitted to the hospital for an attempted suicide. Of course, I prayed that God would relieve him of all his anxiety, stress, and despair. Part of me wanted a quick fix. My heart ached for him. My heart ached for his parents who waited outside his hospital room in the hallway, hoping that I would be able to uncover what had prompted their son to attempt to take his own life. On one hand, they brought him into this world. On the other hand, they lost the ability to provide the care he needed and had to rely on mental health experts to find the systemic causes of his hopelessness. My heart also ached for the boy as I watched him lie in the bed with his wrists shackled to the bed rails. The doctors deemed him a major risk to himself.

I asked, "Would you like to talk?" He shook his head in the affirmative. I asked, "Is there anything you would like to talk about?"

He responded, "Soccer."

"Soccer," I repeated. "Do you like soccer?"

He shook his head in affirmation.

"What position do you play?"

He shrugged his shoulders, and he turned his head away from me. I could see tears streaming down his face. He maneuvered his shoulders to try to dry them, but his shoulders couldn't reach his cheeks because his hands were shackled.

I tried to ignore the tears for a moment and continued with the questioning. "So, you like soccer, but it seems that when I asked you what position you played, you didn't want to tell me. Is that so?"

"Goalie," he said softly.

"Goalie. That's an important position."

He shook his head and the tears flowed.

"Is it something about playing goalie that has upset you?"

He didn't respond. More tears flowed.

I allowed silence to envelop us for about five minutes. I interrupted the silence, "Would you like to tell me how it feels to be a goalie?"

He nodded his head but didn't answer. More tears.

On the nightstand beside his bed, I saw a box of tissues. More time elapsed. We sat in the uncomfortable quiet. I could hear his mother sobbing in the hallway and the father pacing. I started to feel that I had to "fix their son" and give them some reason as to why he wanted to commit suicide. I struggled to navigate my own need to be consoled with his and their need to be consoled. He cried more and struggled to dry the tears with his shoulders. Finally, I asked him, "Would you like me to use a tissue to dry your tears?"

"No. No thank you," he said.

"Would you like to talk about how you are feeling at this moment?"

"Yes."

"Okay. Feel free to tell me what you want me to know. How

are you feeling at this moment?"

"Like a loser. I let the game-winning goal in. I let down my parents. They probably hate me."

"Why do you think they hate you?"

"Because I always let them down. Today it was soccer. Yesterday it was math. I am just a loser. Tomorrow it will be something else."

"Did they tell you they were disappointed in your game today?"

"They didn't have to. As soon as the ball went into the back of the net, I could see them walk away from the field and they waited in the car for me."

"What normally happens after a game?"

"We shake hands with the other team. Our coach talks to us and then as a team we share snacks that one of the parents brought for the day."

"Do your parents usually stay for the snacks or do they always go to the car?"

"When we win and if I have a good game, they stay. Every time we lose or I have a bad game, they leave before the teams are finished shaking hands."

"What happens when you finally get into the car with them?"

"Dead silence. I can tell they are mad and disappointed."

"Do they ever mention the game?"

"Yes, usually a day or two later."

"What do they say?"

"They tell me if I don't work harder, then I will be a loser for the rest of my life. It's the same thing if I bring home a grade lower than an A or if I miss curfew or if I do anything wrong."

"Do you feel that they want you to be perfect?"

"Yes."

"Do you think anyone is actually perfect?"

He shook his head *no* and began to cry. At that point, his parents entered the room and said, "You've had enough time with Kevin. What's wrong with him?"

I paused to respond and by the time I was ready to offer a word, they said, "Never mind. You can just leave now."

My feelings got the better of me, and anger surged. I wanted to defend Kevin by going on the offensive. I felt that the parents had invaded the session and felt they were attempting to bully me out of the room. Therefore, I sternly suggested that we go somewhere private to discuss Kevin's situation. They refused and said, "There's nothing we need from you. Kevin just needs to toughen up and stop this nonsense."

They were becoming heated and Kevin drifted off into a shell of silence. I felt that if I stayed any longer, I would make the situation worse for Kevin. I departed the room, fuming in my anger. I wrote my report and recommended family therapy.

I knew that as much as I wanted to "fix" Kevin and make all his troubles go away, I realized I could not. However, I did console him during the brief time I met with him. It was obvious that his parents were the systemic cause of Kevin's mental health issues, but in a sense, I should have attempted to console them, too.

If I am honest with myself, I resented Kevin's parents and did not see them as my neighbor. They too needed help, serious help. As much as I wanted to help Kevin and console him, I wanted more to somehow bring "justice" to his parents and punish them. Once his parents entered the room and I became an adversary to them, I no longer was able to console Kevin or them. My ability to make a difference hinged on my ability to recognize everyone in the room as my neighbor. I lost my sense of humility and my sight that everyone holds within them the image of God. I lost focus of what was truly important, which was the mental health of Kevin. However, the only way I could care for Kevin was through engaging with his parents in the most positive way possible. I allowed my own need to "save" and "fix" Kevin get in the way. Instead, I failed to see that along with Kevin's suffering his parents, too, were suffering. I took the simple route and wrote them off as cold, uncaring, and self-centered people who were trying to live vicariously through their son. I allowed my need to be angry to become more important for this family's need to be consoled. Somehow in the end, anger was my consolation. I felt justified, thinking I had done everything I was supposed to do.

Unfortunately, I failed in three major areas. First, I lacked humility. If we look at St. Francis' example of "his deep love of humility," then we can witness that he "went among the lepers and remained with them." He was present in their suffering. He was there for them, not for himself. Second, I failed to remain in the purpose of my calling. St. Francis served the lepers "diligently for the love of God." I, on the other hand, became self-serving when I justified my own anger and resentment toward the parents. This emotional response to their failure led me to fail Kevin. In addition, I entirely ignored that my ministry as a chaplain possessed the sole purpose to reveal "the love of God." Third, I lacked the wherewithal in that "brief space" of time and place "to become an evangelical physician and the true healer of souls." I had the opportunity and due to my own selfish need to justify my anger, I threw it away. Perhaps, the reality is that I couldn't do anything there on that day. However, I could have begun the planting of the seeds of renewal. I could have engaged Kevin's parents in the same manner I engaged Kevin by asking questions and allowing them to open up to me. So instead of embracing them as my neighbors, I engaged them as my enemy. The result ended up being counterproductive. I anchored myself to my own insecurities through anger and resentment, giving me a false sense of righteous indignation. Consequently, I failed to see that they also needed healing in mind, body, and spirit.

The question "what do you want me to do for you?" would have been just as beneficial to Kevin's parents as it was for Kevin. However, upon reflection, I believed, at the time, the only way to advocate for Kevin was through the unpeaceful manner of anger and resentment. I have to admit that allowing those two feelings to surface and to become manifested in the room made me feel good. However, the feeling dissipated quickly as I realized I would never see Kevin or his parents again because I unwittingly reinforced the walls they had built around themselves and that I had built around myself. As a result, I have no idea what ever happened to Kevin after that day all because I failed to *seek that it was more important to console rather than be consoled.*

Scriptural Application: Mark 10:51

By the time Jesus and his disciples arrived in Jericho, Jesus' reputation as a healer had reached the people there. They welcomed him and escorted him and his disciples out of the oldest city in the world when he decided to depart. Jesus offered blessings to young children, offered healing and comfort to the sick, offered instruction on what a rich man must do to receive eternal life, and offered a glimpse into the future by foretelling of his death and resurrection. One can say the trip to Jericho resulted in successful ministry. However, that paints the big picture and falls short of explaining the interpersonal interactions between Jesus and the people.

As Jesus leaves the city with a large crowd following him, Bartimaeus shouts to Jesus, asking for mercy. A blind beggar exhibits the faith to just shout out Jesus' name. Even as the crowd tries to shush him, he still cries out.

Before we examine the interactions between Bartimaeus and Jesus, I want to focus on the crowd's reaction to Jesus' visit then their subsequent response to Bartimaeus. Somehow, they seem to have missed the overall message of Jesus' ministry. I wonder why they try to quiet Bartimaeus. Are they embarrassed that a blind beggar, a marginalized person, would be so rude as to shout out to their honored guest? Is Bartimaeus someone they did not want Jesus to see? Did the crowd truly understand that Jesus' message that all people would be saved? Did they fail to realize that Jesus expanded the definition of neighbor to make it universally inclusive? Did they miss the point that Jesus' healing of mind, body, and spirit is a free gift for all people? Their attempts to keep Bartimaeus away from Jesus reminds me of some policies that were enacted by the City Council a few years ago to "clean up the homeless problem in our city." The aim of the motion focused on the tourist district of the city in which the police would round up the homeless people and relocate them to another part of the city. This way, the homeless would not present an eyesore for visitors or scare tourists away. Officials feared that the "homeless problem" would negatively affect tourism and give our city a bad name. The problem with this motion is that it lacked compassion for the homeless individuals and failed to address the systemic cause of homelessness in one of our major cities. In essence, the leadership reflected the actions of the crowd in Jericho, which simply wanted to conceal the blind beggar who actually has a name, Bartimaeus.

The story of Blind Bartimaeus refuses to allow us to dehumanize him like we dehumanize so many of the marginalized people in our midst. Bartimaeus has a name. He has a family. He has a community. Mark refuses to allow us to cast him in an abstract manner as "the blind man" or "the beggar" or "the man over there creating a commotion." No, Mark gives him a name, which implies a personal respect that Jesus will offer Bartimaeus even when no one else will.

Much to the crowd's chagrin, Jesus stops and says, "Call him here." Jesus refuses to allow Bartimaeus to exist on the margins of society. Jesus calls him and welcomes him into the center of the action. Bartimaeus, in his excitement, springs up and throws off his coat. He goes to Jesus.

Jesus makes no assumptions about the man or his needs. As the crowd refuses to console Bartimaeus, Jesus uses it as a teachable moment. Jesus in his tenderness and mercy ask Bartimaeus, "What do you want me to do for you?" In terms of offering another human being care, this question becomes essential in demonstrating respect, trust, and dignity. First, Jesus respects Bartimaeus enough to invite him into close proximity. They come face to face and have a conversation. Second, Jesus trusts Bartimaeus enough that he listens to Bartimaeus explain what he needs. Jesus understands that Bartimaeus doesn't need another person to identify what he needs. Bartimaeus is quite capable of determining his own needs. Third, Jesus illustrates the dignity that should be afforded to every human being. The dignity is reflected in Jesus' empowering Bartimaeus to go and making the point that his faith made him well. In other words, Bartimaeus' faith is just as powerful as all the people of Jericho who enjoyed the benefits of Jesus' ministry.

In essence, Jesus demonstrates how important it is for us to console rather than be consoled. The people of Jericho were consoled by Jesus and they failed to offer the same to Bartimaeus as if his need was not as important as their needs. I find it interesting that Bartimaeus addresses Jesus as a teacher in this episode as if he himself knew that Jesus would offer a teachable moment for all the people witnessing this miracle. On one hand, the miracle rests on the fact that Bartimaeus receives his sight again and follows Jesus on the way. On the other hand, the miracle becomes a final revelation that the people of Jericho failed to understand the inclusive nature of Jesus' ministry *to seek to console rather than be consoled.* In the end, Bartimaeus enjoys the radical beginning of new life, a new life in Christ, and, as a result, follows Jesus clearly. Sadly, in the end it is the people from the center of town who are truly blind to Jesus' teaching and ministry.

Questions for Further Discussion

1. What are the methods in which we can create room in our hearts to console others?

2. Who are those in our lives who we find it difficult to embrace as our neighbor and easy to engage as our enemy?

3. What are our blind spots with regards to ministry? Who do we want to keep quiet or to keep hidden?

4. How have we shown faith so that we can "Go ... and follow Jesus on the way?"

To Understand

The prayer reminds us that we must be willing to understand others; therefore, we may need to stop worrying about winning an argument, trying to prove ourselves right when our focus should be on righteousness. We may need to stop worrying about being the smartest person in the room – the one with all the right answers when we should be listening to one another. We may need to stop worrying about our reputation when we should be more concerned with truth and justice even if we have to admit we are wrong.

When I was younger, I was so concerned about offering sage advice that I often missed the point of many conversations. Instead of listening to the other person, I focused on what I wanted to say. I remember one colleague in grad school who called me out on this a few times. Often times, her frustration grew when I began finishing her sentences in order to move her along so I could present what I wanted to say. For me, I focused more on being understood rather than focusing on trying to understand my colleague.

As one can imagine, I missed many opportunities to engage fully with my colleague and other people. This need to be understood potentially cost me lifelong friendships. Afterall, the message I gave centered on my need to be understood and communicated that I felt no empathy or obligation to listen to the other person. However, this didn't completely hinder my relationships because my ability to become the life of the party endeared me to others. Consequently, people were willing to endure my flaw as long as I could make them laugh. In all reality though, this personal flaw only provided a cover for superficial relationships that did not enter the realm of intimacy and interdependence.

Thank goodness that in the course of time, people who care will point out such character flaws. Also, professional development and coursework also offered a view into this reality. I remember one of the most valuable educational opportunities ever afforded to me was a week-long seminar on counseling. Fortunately, this opportunity came to me early in my career. My then boss recognized both my potential and blind spots as a school leader. As a result, he recommended this week-long course that took place in one of the most beautiful places in the world: Fountain Valley, Colorado. The course was an introduction to counseling. We learned about the benefits of active listening, therapeutic philosophies, and psychological theories all presented through case studies. The course also offered many opportunities to roleplay.

The course changed my view on the world and due to the environment of the desert, I had time to think and reflect not only on what I was learning but on how I needed to improve the quality of my life in order to be a good person. In reality, each morning as I walked or ran through the trails around the complex, I contemplated my relationships with my wife and my sons, my in-laws, my friends, my colleagues, and ultimately with God. Where was I going? What would tomorrow bring? What did God want me to do with the rest of my life? I prayed, not prayers full of words, but prayers that required a true soul scrubbing experience. I prayed for open ears and an open heart. I prayed for understanding. Finally, I wanted to understand others. I would sit on a rock and face Pike's Peak which was off in the distance and just reflect, contemplate, and listen. I am sure the beauty of the place created a setting conducive to listening. I returned home a new person. I felt prepared to help people by listening to them, listening to their thoughts, pains, inner torments. I felt no need to "fix" them. I only wanted to give them an ear of empathy and compassion. I finally realized how much more important it was to understand than to be understood. This reality provided me with another opportunity to enjoy a radical beginning. The idea behind understanding others sits in the reality of being present, fully present and engaged. In essence, I learned that at times I had to make myself small in order to serve the needs of others. To paraphrase John the Baptist, *I must decrease so that Jesus may increase.*

Scriptural Application: Proverbs 18: 2

Ever since part of my ministry has focused on Haiti, I have fallen in love with proverbs. The people of Haiti can boast of over 1200 proverbs unique to their culture. They are pearls of wisdom that shed light on their history, theology, struggles, core values, and hope. Some are easy to understand. For example, the simplicity of *little by little, straw by straw, a bird builds her nest* reveals the patience one needs to possess when creating something good and safe. Others are enigmatic. For example, the meaning *words in the belly don't rot the guts* remains allusive and inaccessible.

My love for Haitian proverbs prompted me to read and study the Book of Proverbs, which was a book I avoided because it lacked a narrative structure. However, I developed a relevant purpose for reading The Book of Proverbs and discovered some real gems. The ones that spoke to me, I wrote on index cards and set them to memory. Not so much to offer them as "pearls of wisdom" at an opportune time but more as guides for how I should act or behave as a leader. For example, "Know well the condition of your flock and give attention to your herds; for riches do not last forever, nor a crown for all generations" (27: 23-24). One can imagine why it would be necessary for any church leader in any given context to follow this sage advice. Simply put, as leaders, we must come to know our direct reports, our congregation, and our constituents as intimately as possible in order to serve them as Jesus served the recipients of his ministry. These "riches" of our ministry "or [the] crown" of our authority will not last "for all generations." We have a window of opportunity to lead by serving and to serve by leading. Therefore, we must make it our aim to know the people who are the beneficiaries of our service.

Perhaps my favorite proverb that relates well to Francis' maxim is *to seek to understand rather than to be understood.* "A fool takes no pleasure in understanding, but only in expressing personal opinion" (Proverbs 18:2).

This proverb has so much relevance not only for my personal and professional relationships but is also poignant for the divisions that exist in our small communities, our country, and the world. Our sense of civility has been lost. Our need to understand one another has been discarded like old shoes.

Often times, before I enter a meeting, I take a deep breath and recite this proverb. I now have no need to sound as if everything I say has to be sagacious or astute. I don't feel such pressure anymore. Perhaps I have become more comfortable in my skin over the last twenty-five years or so. Nevertheless, I know that I am at my best in professional meetings and in one-on-one dialogues when I listen and seek to understand the other people's positions. This doesn't mean that I am not able to possess a point of view and this doesn't mean that I am not permitted to disagree with someone else. What it means for me is that I don't need to look at my conversations as debates that I need to win. I look at these conversations as dialogues with the aim where both parties or all the parties involved may gain new insights.

I've learned over the years that everyone maintains a

perspective of the world. People come at an issue from different starting points. For example, one time when a Jewish colleague and I were walking across our campus, she commented that she didn't like our chapel. Initially, she caught me off-guard because the chapel was my favorite building on campus. Fortunately, I put myself into a pastoral role and asked *why* because I truly wanted to understand her perspective. She explained, "Because the cross is right in your face." (Note: the cross that sits upon the steeple can be seen even before one enters our campus.) I asked her to enlighten me regarding her feeling about the cross. "Well, as a Jewish person, it represents a long history of bigotry, anti-Semitism, and hatred. As a Jewish woman, I can't help but think of the ages of persecution our people suffered in the name of that cross. For me, it is an evil symbol." She expressed this viewpoint – her world view on the cross – without anger and without resentment. Afterall, she knew I was Christian, and she knew I was a priest. She didn't hold back any punches.

I thanked her for her honesty and for sharing her thoughts, and I responded, "It's amazing how one symbol can have two different responses from two people who share many of the same values. I never realized the pain caused by our most sacred symbol. However, I am glad that I now know." We went on to discuss how Jews suffered at the hands of Christians ever since the second century. By listening to one another, we came to an understanding where mutual respect, honesty, and accountability forge the strong bond of interpersonal relationships. I discovered on that day that two people don't need to agree on everything but only need to respect one another enough to be willing *to take pleasure in understanding.*

Questions for Further Discussion

1. How would your colleagues, friends, and family explain your ability to understand them?
2. Describe a time when you truly listened to someone else and explain how it helped your relationship. How did the conversation make you feel?
3. Explain the dangers of our need to be right.
4. Can you think of other scriptural passages that highlight the importance of listening or focusing on understanding?

To Love

Now, in order to experience authentic love, we must focus more on the love we give than the love we receive. Love isn't granted in order to gain anything. True love is given freely and with the grace not to expect anything in return. With that said, we all need love. We need to feel beloved by another person. However, that's not where the power of love lives. The power of love exists in giving love away. Unlike material goods, love grows within us the more we share it. Consequently, when we share our resources, our resources tend to diminish. This is not the case with love.

When I was a boy, I never knew my grandparents. However, my best friend's grandparents became my surrogate grandparents. Tommy and I would occasionally walk to his grandparents' house for short visits. We knew we were guaranteed a treat or a quarter that we could spend at the corner store. However, we loved to listen to Pop-Pop's stories. He would share stories about his childhood, his time in the Navy, and his life as a house painter. His stories always focused on doing good, working hard, and leading a clean life.

As Tommy and I grew older, we tended to join other crowds of kids, leaving our relationship to the realm of simple acquaintance. However, I kept my relationship with Pop-Pop and

Granny. I continued to visit them. By the time I was a teenager, Granny's health began to decline. This was the first time that I saw selfless love in action. Pop-Pop took over all the cleaning, cooking, and shopping. He did it all. He showed great tenderness to Granny when he brushed her hair or lifted her up from her chair to walk her to the dinner table. He cooked her favorite foods, talked to her in a lilting voice, and gave her baths. Pop-Pop never complained. His outward actions reflected the inward love of his heart. At this point in their marriage, he did not receive much in return. Granny wasn't able to speak to him, initiate touch, or do anything on her own. She became completely dependent on Pop-Pop. He never lost the gleam in his eye when he looked at Granny. He would share stories with me about their early years of courtship, and he would include Granny in the conversation by saying, "Remember that, Granny?" She would slowly turn her head and offer a slight smile. I think her smile became a treasure for him.

She eventually passed away. I visited him. I saw for the first time in my life grief, a grief that was palpable. I would inquire how he was holding up, and he would respond, "I miss her dearly," and his voice would crack. Tears would fill his eyes and he would add, "You know, Tim, I would not change anything." To me as a young teenager, that was the first time I witnessed love in totality. I learned from Pop-pop that love wasn't a feeling. It was a commitment. It was a commitment to meeting the needs of the other person even if there was no guarantee of return payback. I learned that the love given was the payback itself. The gift of love is only love when it is given away.

Scriptural Application: Genesis— Jacob and Rachel
Of all of the love stories in The Bible, I am continually

drawn to the story of Jacob and Rachel. After Jacob flees the wrath of his brother, Esau, he ends up in his kinfolk's home. He sees Rachel. Love at first sight. He seeks permission from Laban to marry her, which Jacob receives, but he must work for seven years. The cost of love. After the seven years end, Laban dupes Jacob into marrying Leah. Jacob is furious. However, Laban offers him Rachel once again but first Jacob must work another seven years on Laban's farm. Jacob so loves Rachel that he is willing to see beyond the present moment and the price he must pay to obtain that love. His love for Rachel is undeterred. He does what it takes to show his love for her. True love is the greatest motivator in our world.

God's love for the world supersedes all other loves. God so loves the world that he gives his only son. Jesus knew the mission of the Father. He also knew that the mission of his father was his own mission. He was in the Father and the Father was in him. Jesus also knew that all who would abide in him would also abide in the Father and the Father would be in them. Love is the common denominator in all healthy relationships. God's relationship with the world is based on love. Our relationship with God likewise is based on love. However, what we learn from God is that love is only love when it is given away. God can't love humankind without giving his breath to us, giving creation to us, and giving his only son to us.

Jesus constantly gives himself to his disciples and invites the entire world to partake in the free gift of salvation that Jesus offers through the willing self-sacrifice he makes on the cross. Jesus reminds his disciples that there is "no greater gift than to lay down one's life for a friend." However, how we lay down our life for a friend or loved one may require us not so much to die a physical death but to die to our own needs in order to put the needs of others first. In practical matters, we will not always be granted the opportunity to offer our life to another by dying a physical death. Therefore, we may find that we must surrender our own needs or wants in order to support someone else's needs or wants. For example, I am sure that Pop-Pop would have loved to go to the corner bar and share a beer with friends like he did in his younger days. However, he knew that he couldn't leave Granny alone. Granny's needs became his needs. Jesus' need to give us salvation is more about our need for salvation. God gives his only son to the world in order to show his love for the world. God doesn't condemn the world but sends Christ into the world to bring salvation to all. Sadly, the only way Jesus was capable of bringing salvation to the world was through his suffering and dying on the cross.

Jesus did not *so much seek to be loved as to love.* Pop-Pop also lived into this Christian reality of love. He knew after many years of marriage that it was more important to love than to be loved. In the end, if we are to maximize God's gift of love to the world, we must realize that the only way for that to happen is to love our neighbor, which includes our enemies. We must remember that God loves everyone. Therefore, we should, too.

In closing, 1 John 4 states,

"We love because [God] first loved us. Those who say, "I love God," and hate their brothers or sisters, are liars; for those who do not love a brother or sister whom they have seen, cannot love God whom they have not seen. The commandment we have from [Christ] is this: those who love God must love their brothers and sisters also."

John clearly reminds us that the only way we can love God is by loving others. God gave us Christ, his only son, to demonstrate this command to love others. We may remember from Luke's Gospel that Jesus says, as the men hammer nails into his hands, "Father, forgive them for they know not what they are doing." In essence, Jesus, at the moment of great vulnerability and through selfless love, asks God to forgive those who demonstrate the greatest hate through torture and murder. Jesus shows love even when no one expects it. This is so the world will profit from this singular act of love.

Questions for Further Discussion
1. *Who in your life exemplifies love?*
2. *How does your faith community demonstrate Christian love?*
3. *When in your life have you been the recipient of selfless love?*
4. *When in your life have you given selfless love?*

Chapter 5

Sowing Seeds for Eternal Life

The Fourth Movement: Towards an Eternal Life

Finally, we arrive at the Fourth Movement of the prayer. *It is in giving that we receive* leads us to the reality that peace generates a heart of mercy where we perform acts of charity promptly, diligently, and frequently. According to Francis de Sales, this marks the life of a devout Christian. Once again doing for others without profiting from our works. The prayer reminds us that it is in pardoning that we are pardoned – this echoes the Lord's Prayer – "forgive us as we forgive others". Perhaps we need to show some grace and give each other the benefit of the doubt. Wherever we live, we must develop a culture where we can pardon others even when it doesn't make sense. Furthermore, "we must love because God first loved us." Love leads us to our radical beginning, the root to who we truly are, which draws us to love God and neighbor. Love is the keystone to all the other virtues expressed in the Prayer Attributed to St. Francis. Ultimately, love delivers us from selfish need. We die to gain eternal life. Once we die to self, then we become eternally bound with God in the same manner as Jesus and God are one.

Giving

I can't think of a time when I have known a person who engaged in some type of service that the person did not come away from the work feeling somewhat joyful. I have taken students, teachers, and parents into urban areas to feed the homeless. I have given people opportunities to serve at a nursing home or a marginalized school. I have taken people to the remote, rural areas of Haiti. Each time, the people who serve feel they gained more than the beneficiaries of their service. We do truly receive when we give.

One time, a student who was struggling with minor depression and some self-esteem issues came to me on a regular basis for counseling. She was a top student at an elite independent school and failed to see how her academic success should bring satisfaction. She failed to see how the medals and trophies she earned as a runner should bring her happiness. Intellectually, she realized that she should be happy. She came from a loving family with all the material things a person could need. She attended the best sports and academic camps during the summer. She excelled in science, language, and the arts. She sang solos in the church choir and played the cello. In her mind, she knew that she should be happy, but she wasn't. She walked around on the verge of tears, trying to figure out who she was supposed to be. She felt trapped by her success, and it didn't make her feel good about herself. She beat herself up because she wasn't happy. Her sadness resembled a great pit in which the more she tried to climb out of it the more the walls just crumbled around her. Nevertheless, she faithfully came each week to meet with me to work through her self-loathing.

One day, I asked, "What do you want?"

"What do you mean?" She asked.

I paused and tried to reframe the question. "You say over and over that you have everything a person could want, but you are still unhappy. Straight A's and fast running times are things you are supposed to do because you are good at them. Playing the cello and singing don't bring you any sense of happiness. You are realizing these activities don't define you. So, if this were a perfect world, what could you do that may help you discover your true self?"

She looked away from me for a moment to process my question. This was the first-time tears didn't fill her eyes. This was the first time she didn't wring her hands as we talked. She took a deep breath and seemed fully relaxed. "Do you know the students who I really admire?"

"No. Tell me."

"The students who don't care about the grades. The students who play sports just because they enjoy being with other kids. I admire that. That's what I want."

"So, what would that look like for you?"

"I'm not sure. I've been thinking about this for a while. I observed that these kids don't seem to be defined by what they do. They just are. They seem comfortable in their own skin. They care but they don't seem to care what others say or think about them."

"That's an astute observation."

"Also, they don't seem to care if they receive accolades for what they do. They just do and that seems to bring them joy. That's what I want."

I nodded my head in agreement and asked again, "So what does that look like for you? In other words, what would make you comfortable in your own skin? What activity could you do so the activity itself becomes the reward?"

"I've been reading about Gandhi, and this one quote seems to hit home. I'm not sure if he actually said it, but it resonates with me."

"Tell me the quote."

"The best way to find yourself is to lose yourself in the service of others." After reading about his life, I just come to the realization that my talents seem to focus me on taking. I know that I earn my academic awards and athletic accolades, but I don't see how these things benefit others. When I walk up to the stage to receive a certificate because I broke the mile record, I feel empty inside. I feel like I am only doing what I am able to do just like other kids, but I am being rewarded for it because of an arbitrary time. I wonder, 'Where is the substance in all of this?'"

I let her question linger and paused for a few minutes. Finally, I said, "What would you like to do?"

"Serve. I want to serve other people. It doesn't matter what I do as long as I can lose myself in service to others."

We developed a plan of service to see what would fall into her wheelhouse. First, she served at the soup kitchen. We debriefed to see how she felt about the experience. For the first time she felt a sense of true joy and satisfaction because she gave her time and attention to other people without being rewarded for it. She sensed that the people she served who could be classified as the poorest of the poor, the homeless and destitute, felt more gratitude for the little they received than her classmates who benefited from a life of abundance. Ultimately, she discovered other service opportunities where her academic and athletic skills could benefit other people. She tutored at an urban after-school program and volunteered for the Special Olympics.

In the end, even though she still struggled with mild depression, her self-esteem rose in conjunction with the service she offered other people. The service opportunities gave her a sense of purpose beyond herself. As a person, she no longer viewed herself as competing with other students. She saw that what she learned in the classroom could eventually help other people. Even as a distance runner, she came to understand that even that gift could be used to benefit her teammates and even her opponents. She now intuitively understood that in *giving we receive.*

Scriptural Application: 2 Corinthians 9: 6 – 9

Yes, this young woman reaped the harvest of her own giving and the more she gave the more she reaped. *It is in giving that we receive.* However, we can't give grudgingly. Our giving must come from the heart. In order to receive from our giving, we must not expect anything in return, nor can we attach strings to our giving. Our giving to others can't be transactional. Our giving must be based on grace. Paul understands this when he is writing to the Corinthians, encouraging them to be generous. Paul ministers with a sense of urgency and expectation of Jesus' second coming and desires for all people to be saved, especially the poor. Therefore, he focuses on collecting money for that purpose. Paul speaks to the heart of the matter and the true spirit of generosity when he states:

"The point is this: the one who sows sparingly will also reap sparingly, and the one who sows bountifully will also reap bountifully. Each of you must give as you have made up your mind, not reluctantly or under compulsion, for God loves a cheerful giver. And God is able to provide you with every blessing in abundance, so that by always having enough of everything, you may share abundantly in every good work. As it is written,

"He scatters abroad, he gives to the poor; his righteousness endures forever" (2 Corinthians 9: 6 – 9).

Just as the young girl in the scenario above, when she sows sparingly, she reaped sparingly. She worked hard in all she did, but the end results only benefited her. Therefore, her "accomplishments" actually made her feel less of a person rather than someone who was part of something greater than herself. When she sowed bountifully, sharing her talents and giving her time to others, she reaped bountifully. Once she "lost herself in service to others," she realized that "God loves a cheerful giver" and received "blessings in abundance." In reality, she committed herself to serve others and she "made up her mind" to give "not reluctantly or under compulsion" but from a true spirit of generosity.

Interestingly enough, when she accomplished excellence in academics and sports without regard for others, she did the work reluctantly and under compulsion because that's what others expected of her. The awards, medals, and accolades became the goal of the work. The work itself brought very little reward, if any at all. However, her service work became the reward itself. The relationships she built tutoring a child or serving at the soup kitchen made her a cheerful giver because in the end, she realized that it *is in giving that she received.*

Questions

1. *Tell of a time when you performed service work. Explain how you felt before, during and after the service work.*
2. *What does it mean to be a cheerful giver?*
3. *How do our children define themselves? What is our role in helping them define themselves?*
4. *How do you discern how God calls you to service?*

Pardoning

The fourth movement continues with *it is in pardoning that we are pardoned.* Perhaps one could argue that the only condition God places upon us to receive God's grace is dependent upon the grace we give to others. The idea that we ask God to *forgive us as we forgive others* demands of us that we keep expanding our hearts to practice more and more mercy. When we pardon another person, we, in reality, pardon ourselves. I know from personal experience that holding grudges only imprisons me and holds me in the tight grip of anxiety, fear, and self-loathing.

The refusal to forgive and the commitment to hold onto a grudge or to seek revenge will have devastating consequences. First, this commitment to withhold pardon and to desire revenge only bring about anxiety. I remember one time as a teenager, I desired to seek revenge on a classmate. I will call the classmate George. George and I hung out with the same group of kids. However, that's where our similarities ended. We fought all of the time. Our fighting ranged from verbal jabs to physical jabs. After I stopped hanging out with that group of teens, one night, with the help of two of "his allies," he tracked me down and we fought. I found myself on the wrong end of a beating. I swore I would enact revenge. I became obsessed with repaying George. Each time I saw him from a distance, I grew anxious because I had not lived up to my self-made promise. I acknowledge that I missed a small window of opportunity when I could catch him off-guard. This failure to take advantage of the situation created in me a heavy fear which I carried with me for days after "the opportunity" had been missed. I feared George as more time separated the present from the night of our last encounter. I wanted revenge but didn't know how to go about it due to the reality that he was older, stronger, and faster than I was. Finally, this failure to offer pardon and to seek revenge only led to self-loathing. George was in my head and he didn't even know he was there. Nevertheless, I started to loathe myself because I saw myself as a coward.

This cycle of anxiety, fear, and self-loathing continued for about a year. I finally went to confession and dumped all of this "baggage" onto the lap of Father Hanlon, my eleventh-grade history teacher. He explained that the only way for me to receive pardon, and ultimately peace, was to offer pardon. In essence, he told me to surrender. This seemed so counterintuitive to everything I had learned growing up, but it seemed that at that moment I was so controlled by anxiety, fear, and self-loathing that I wanted to do anything to escape these feelings. I explained to Father Hanlon how I had planned to jump George from behind and catch him by surprise. Or how I had planned to surprise him by jumping out of an alley when he was walking down the street. I shared other plans of revenge. He finally said, "Tim, you have spent so much thought, time, and energy on this that it seems to me that you have become victim to the image you created of George and to the fantasy you have created for yourself to somehow subdue him." I just listened, and then he added, "I am sure George doesn't even give you any thought whatsoever. He has moved on and you have remained trapped in the darkness of your last encounter."

"So, what do you suggest?" I asked.

"I suggest that instead of clinging to the darkness of that night, you go deep into your heart and find the strength and courage to simply forgive him. You don't need him to ask for forgiveness. You simply find it in your heart to forgive. I believe that when you do that, you will feel liberated."

I pondered the wisdom of Fr. Hanlon for a few days. I figured this was a man of great courage, a man who had fought in World

War II and taught in one of the toughest areas of Philadelphia. I assumed he knew what he was talking about. I gave his advice a chance.

I went to our school's tiny chapel in the basement of the main building. I knelt before the altar and asked God to give me the strength and courage to forgive George and to free me from this desire to seek revenge. At that moment, I felt a certain lightness within and felt a liberation from the torment that weighed heavy upon me each day I failed to enact revenge. Pardon brought peace and I felt pardoned from anxiety, fear, and self-loathing.

Scriptural Application: Luke 23: 26 - 42

Forgiveness is a gift that we not only give to others but a gift we give ourselves. When we forgive, we free others from a debt to us. In addition, when we forgive, we free ourselves from the manacles of resentment, hostility, fear, anxiety, self-loathing and a host of other psychological barriers that prevent us from becoming who we truly are meant to be.

Throughout the Gospels, Jesus speaks of forgiveness. In matter of fact, the primary message of the Gospel is forgiveness. Forgiveness leads to personal and interpersonal transformation. Forgiveness allows and nurtures a radical beginning, a beginning where acceptance, reconciliation, and love become the keystone of our relationships with one another and with God. Forgiveness lays the foundation for a future where the world can become the kingdom which God intended. If we examine the scriptures and its central focus on forgiveness, we will make sense of why Jesus willingly died for our sins.

When the apostles ask Jesus how many times we should forgive someone who offends us, they offer an answer, which is seven times. Jesus takes that much further in one traditional translation and responds, "No, not seven times, but seventy times seven." This response recalls Psalm 90 which states life expectancy is seventy years. So, I see Jesus' response to how many times we must forgive another person is seven lifetimes' worth. In other words, no limit can be set on how often we must forgive.

Luke's Gospel develops a compelling scene during Jesus' crucifixion on true forgiveness. Luke writes:

"Two others also, who were criminals, were led away to be put to death with him. When they came to the place that is called The Skull, they crucified Jesus there with the criminals, one on his right and one on his left. Then Jesus said, "Father, forgive them; for they do not know what they are doing." And they cast lots to divide his clothing. And the people stood by, watching; but the leaders scoffed at him, saying, 'He saved others; let him save himself if he is the Messiah of God, his chosen one!'"

Although Jesus is innocent of any crime, he is placed between two criminals. As he is nailed to the cross Jesus says, "Father, forgive them; for they do not know what they are doing." I want to offer two insights into this realization by Jesus. First, I feel that Jesus understood the human condition only as God could – hence Jesus' divine nature is realized during this scene. In essence, Jesus knows that since humans are subject to sin and death, they are not truly conscious of the nature of sin and its effect at the time they commit the sin. How often do we offend someone without truly thinking of its full ramifications on the person, on us, or on the community at large? Somehow, the power of sin blinds us at the moment when we become one with sin. This is not to say we are not responsible for our sin. We are. However, do we truly know what we are doing when we hurt others? In most cases, we believe we are justified by our actions, and the reality in the crucifixion scene demonstrates there is no justification for sin. We learn from Jesus that the only thing for which we can become justified is God's grace: "Father, forgive them; for they do not know what they do." Jesus in his pain and torment realizes the only salve for humanity is grace.

Second, when Jesus says, "forgive them," who are "them?" On first look, he may limit this to the soldiers who are nailing him to the cross. After all, they just follow orders. However, this seems to miss the point of Jesus crucified. Therefore, he may expand this request to include the Pharisees, Sadducees, and Scribes who manipulated Roman Law in order to secure Jesus' crucifixion. However, this falls short to address who are the "them." Therefore, I believe Jesus seeks forgiveness from God, the Father, for the soldiers who nail him to the cross, to the Jewish leaders who manipulated Roman Law, to the apostles who deserted him, to Judas who betrayed him, to the lukewarm followers who failed to buy into the Gospel, to the criminals hanging on each side of him, and to all of humanity for all time.

If we delve into the New Testament, we find Jesus illustrating the importance of forgiveness when he tells the Parable of the Unforgiving Servant who, due to his callous heart, refuses to forgive his subordinate a debt even though his much greater debt was forgiven. He suffers, not due to his own debt or sin, but due to his refusal to forgive another person. Jesus alludes to the forgiveness of sin during the Sermon on the Mount and Sermon on the Plain. He calls for his followers to develop hearts of mercy. He encourages them to love their enemies. In addition, to the great sermons, Jesus in many of his parables explains the power of forgiveness and how it leads to a radical beginning in a life turned over to God. In the Parable of the Pharisee and the Tax

Collector, we see "the sinner" coming away justified because he seeks forgiveness. In the Parable of the Prodigal Son, the younger son receives forgiveness from the father without asking. The forgiveness leads to restoration, or a radical beginning where things can start new and the forgiven person now possesses the opportunity to become free from sin in order to be right with God.

In the end, as Jesus hangs on the cross, we see soldiers gambling for his clothes and hear the leaders scoff at him, saying, "He saved others; let him save himself if he is the Messiah of God, his chosen one!" However, they miss the point. Jesus knows this willing gesture of sacrifice leads to saving others. Sadly, those who gamble for his clothes and those who scoff at him fail to understand that they are the beneficiaries of Jesus' crucifixion. In the end, Jesus does not wait for people to repent. Jesus proactively forgives. God calls us to expand our hearts of mercy so that we, too, can proactively pardon others.

Questions

1. *Why is the free offering of forgiveness so difficult for us?*
2. *Can you think of a time when you were forgiven by someone?*
3. *Can you think of a time when you found it difficult to forgive yourself?*
4. *Can you think of a time when you forgave someone proactively?*

Eternal Life

And the prayer concludes: *it is in dying that we are born to eternal life.* In our culture, we tend to think that death is what happens at end of life. However, when we are in right-relationship with God, accept the faith of Jesus Christ, and enter into the advocacy of the Holy Spirit, then we enter into eternal life of the seamless relationship of the Trinity. Furthermore, when we are in right-relationship with others, we often have to die to our selfish needs in order for our relationships to grow and flourish. It is in dying to self that we are born into a life with others. When we die to ourselves, we open an entirely whole new life for others and paradoxically a whole new life for ourselves. We discover our radical beginning. We become who we are meant to be: the image of God on earth.

We can die to our selfish needs and find a radical beginning where we can start afresh, start new where peace is not just a goal but a way of life – a way of life in which we come to know ourselves fully, come to embrace the reality that we need one another, and come to recognize our purpose is to glorify God. In the end, the Prayer of St. Francis is addressed to God, asking God to help us to become more fully embraced in our own humanity.

As Christians, we embrace not only the teachings of Jesus Christ, but we also enter into faith that is founded on the actions of Christ and not our own actions. We enter eternal life because we believe in the grace of God given to us through the atoning actions of Jesus Christ. When Jesus prays for his disciples in chapter seventeen of John's Gospel, he explicitly says, "And this is eternal life, that they may know you, the only true God, and Jesus Christ whom you have sent." We learn early in John's Gospel that God sends Christ into the world to save the world and not to condemn the world so all who believe in Christ will have eternal life. In the end, perhaps the best way to know God leads us to die to self, to perform acts of charity with a cheerful heart, and to allow the image of God in us to embrace the image of God in others. Perhaps this reality leads us to the radical beginning where our internal image of God is the true source of who we truly are.

I started to meditate on the Prayer of Sr. Francis one Christmas Eve when an elderly man asked me to recite it to him for his Christmas Blessing. Perhaps that's how Christ comes to us, on mysterious evenings during pandemics when we are faced with a challenge, as simple as it may seem, that we cannot meet. Perhaps the brokenness of our world can only be healed through the paradox of our failure to rise to a challenge or rise to an occasion to do something simple for someone else. Perhaps the brokenness of our world can only be healed when we come to terms with our own brokenness. Maybe coming to terms with our own brokenness inspires us to die to the self in order to rise up with Christ.

Scriptural Application – Genesis 15

In my youth, I thought eternal life began with death. Eternal life existed outside this world. However, as I study scripture and meditate on God's Holy Word, I have come to understand that eternal life exists in the here and now. It stems from faith.

I love the story of Abraham, especially when God takes Abraham for a walk under the stars and promises him that he will be the father of a great nation. "God brought him outside and said, "Look toward heaven and count the starts, if you are able to count them." At this moment, I am sure Abraham looks up and without light pollution sees a dark canvas of an infinite number of stars. "Then God said to him, 'So shall your descendants be.' And Abraham believed the Lord; and the Lord reckoned it to him as righteousness." At this point in the Abraham story, Abraham hasn't done anything of significance to be recognized by God as righteous. Therefore, Abraham's faith in God's promise makes him righteous. This faith which God reckons as righteous brings Abraham eternal life. We learn from the following scene that eternal life doesn't grant a pain-free life. However, we learn that God's promise is unconditional and extends to all of Abraham's offspring. The subsequent scene may seem obscure, so let's examine it through the ancient custom of making a covenant. In ancient times, when two parties made a covenant, an animal would be sacrificed or cut. The root of the Hebrew word for covenant is *cut* or *KRT*. Therefore, a covenant was cut. The two parties cut an animal carcass in half and laid the pieces side by side with enough room for both parties to walk through it. This act of walking through the animal carcass sealed the covenant. After God reckons Abraham's faith as righteous, God tells Abraham, "to bring me a heifer three years old, a female goat three years old, a ram three years old." The narrative continues, "Abraham brought him all these and cut them in two, laying each half over against the other." After he completes the preparation, Abraham falls into a deep sleep and receives a disturbing revelation that his offspring will suffer four hundred years of enslavement. However, as he comes out of the vision, he sees "a smoking fire pot and a flaming torch passed between these pieces." Abraham never walks through the pieces, nor does God demand him to do so. However, one may conclude that God was the one carrying the pot and torch, and, therefore, had walked through the animal pieces. As a result, God sealed the Covenant, but did not require Abraham to walk through the animal pieces because he knew that even though the Covenant is unconditional, God realizes that Abraham and his offspring would never be able to uphold their part of the agreement. However, God would never break the promise and would uphold the Covenant for eternity.

The final seal of the Covenant comes with Jesus' act of dying on the cross and resurrecting three days later on Easter Sunday. In the end, our entry into eternal life depends not on our actions, but on the actions of God.

Questions for Further Discussion
1. *Explain a time when you completely depended on God the Father, God the Son, or God the Holy Spirit.*
2. *Describe a time when you realized faith possessed more power or impact than your own actions.*
3. *How do you define "eternal life"?*
4. *How does your worship community live out its faith in Christ?*

Epilogue:

We Are Holy Partners in a Heavenly Calling

As I grow older, I become more comfortable with living according to the spirit of the law rather than the letter of the law. I've come to realize "the spirit gives life." Also, I understand that the spirit of the Law is aspirational. Simply put, anyone who is reading this probably can testify to never having murdered anyone. Nevertheless, resisting murder does not make one righteous. If we measure righteousness by things done or left undone, then, as the Apostle Paul claims, we can never claim righteousness as achieved. The reality hinges on the fact that we need God's grace and the faith of Jesus Christ to receive righteousness. We cannot simply create a biblical checklist and provide empirical evidence that we attained righteousness.

I remember in my youth, I believed I could work my way into Heaven or somehow win over God's good graces. This approach to righteousness frustrated me and shaped my resentment toward other people. Also, I saw my spiritual life both as a competition with others and as an individual accomplishment. I held no sense of peace, pardon, or understanding of others. I justified my meanness directed at others if I believed someone else was lazy, weak, or unengaged with my line of thinking.

Therefore, instead of examining and reflecting on the good works that I may do, I pray to God that my heart is full of peace, pardon, love, unity, faith, hope, light, and joy. On my best days I seek to console, to understand, and to love as opposed to seeking consolation, understanding, and love. Since the prayer is aspirational, on my worst days, I have an opportunity to bounce back and offer myself some of the grace and mercy that others deserve. Also, on my bad days – those days when I fall short of living into the Prayer of St. Francis – I realize how dependent I am on God.

I realize the Prayer Attributed to St. Francis calls us into communal living. The prayer and its precepts are not meant just for the individual. Francis realized Christianity embraced the idea and ideal of community. He welcomed a spirit of community and testified that Christ entered the world and its community in order to offer salvation to all people. Through community, we accomplish more than we can on our own. *Many hands make light work,* as my mother liked to say. This prayer draws us closer to God because the prayer calls us to honor the Divine Image in each person we meet. In essence, the prayer recognizes we are "holy partners in a heavenly calling."

I love and minister in a politically diverse community. As a result, many people desire to know where I fall in terms of American politics. I am asked, "Are you a Republican or democrat?" People want to put me into a category so that they can size me up for whatever reason. However, I can just show them the Prayer of St. Francis and say, "Here is my political platform. I'm neither a Republican nor Democrat. I am just a struggling Christian who desires to rest in God's welcoming embrace."

www.ingramcontent.com/pod-product-compliance
Lightning Source LLC
LaVergne TN
LVHW091933070526
838200LV00068B/956